The World Beyond the Window

& Other Stories

by

Chuck Holmes

CS/Books | Atlanta, GA

These stories are works of fiction and, with the exception of certain place names and famous people, any resemblance to actual people, places, or events is purely coincidental.

Published by CS/Books, a part of Corporate Strategies, Inc., Atlanta, GA.

Printed in the United States of America

Cover photograph by Michael Nelson

Library of Congress Cataloging Data is available upon request.

978-1-63684-241-7

Books are available in quantity for book clubs, promotional or premium use. For information, contact info@chuckholmes.org

First Edition, 2020

10 9 8 7 6 5 4 3 2 1

Dedicated to the memory of

Josefina Niggli,

who claimed that she could not teach anyone to write, but could teach us to make a living at it. She was right.

Acknowledgments and Disclaimers

A lot of people contributed their time and wisdom to the selection and development of these stories. They include relatives: Linda, my wife; my brother, Pat; my daughter and son-in-law, Leslie and David Harrington; and long-time friends: Toby Hufham, George and Jeannie Wearn, Jim Maney, and Rich Vurva.

There does need to be a word or so about liberties I've taken with things that really exist, but not in the form presented here. Smithfield is an actual place in North Carolina, and I remember it as a pretty town that felt right for Erin to return to in "The World Beyond the Window." However, since I know no one in Smithfield, I'm certain that all of the characters in the story are fictional. The town also shows up as a destination in "The Spirit of Ava Gardner."

Ava Gardner is from a community named Grabtown, which is evidently little-known in Johnston County, and there is a museum dedicated to her in Smithfield. However, the childhood home depicted in the short story only exists as I imagined it. The characteristics attributed to her spirit in the story are common in articles about the movie star.

Table of Contents

Introduction

Once upon a time, books were simply "books," divided by whether they were fiction or nonfiction. There were a few subcategories, such as detective stories, but for the most part, the writer didn't have to worry about which compartment to squeeze his novel into. I would imagine that Sinclair Lewis would have had some difficulty finding a standard genre for *Arrowsmith,* Fitzgerald for *The Great Gatsby,* or Hemingway for *The Old Man and the Sea.*

However, times have changed, as have the ways that people buy books. Now writers are forced to pick one or more genres or categories so readers can search Amazon, Barnes and Noble, and other platforms. In the position of having to choose, I chose "Religious," knowing that some readers may disagree with me.

That's not only fine, but it's to be expected. Just as I believe that most viewers bring their own meaning to a work of art, I believe that readers bring their own interpretation and meaning to the stories they read. I never did believe that Melville consciously included in Moby Dick all of the symbols listed on the sixty pages handed out to us in the American Novel class. In fact, I imagine that he would have been as surprised as I was at some of them.

Consequently, I'll leave it to the reader to decide whether Morton Findlay, a man who studiously avoids the abrasiveness of the world or Joe Spivey in "One of God's Finest Creations" or any of the other characters here deserves to be in a story that's in a book that calls itself "religious."

I only hope that when you arrive at the end of the story, you'll consider the time you've invested well spent.

Love

When I graduated from seminary, I wished that Baptist ministers wore clerical collars. It was a sign that the wearer had received a special calling, that he was set apart from everyone else. It seemed appropriate. I had declared my vocation. I'd gone to college, then to seminary. I had spent countless hours—either paid or unpaid—working in the church. At the time, it seemed right that I should have some sort of badge of spiritual rank like the Catholics and Episcopalians do.

But that was nine years ago. Now, I'm glad that we don't, not just because I don't want to be seen as a person with a special calling, but because, in my button-down shirt and Dockers, I don't feel quite so much like an imposter.

That thought crossed my mind as I hurried up the sidewalk to Love McKinley's house, wondering what I could say to a family whose wife and mother had committed suicide. Her husband and two grown children had to be bewildered. She was literally here one day and gone the next. She was not old, just about sixty. She didn't have some sort of terminal disease that took her little by little, allowing the family to prepare for it. She didn't perish in a car accident caused by some drunk or distracted driver. She simply took an entire bottle of pain pills while no one was at home.

There were a few neighbors standing in the yard talking when I got to the house, little clots of people, talking in low tones, occasionally glancing toward the house. I slowed down to speak and shake their hands before going into the house.

Somehow, the house smelled of death, stale air trapped in the high-ceilinged rooms, wrapped around the overstuffed furniture. I had never been in this house before, so I didn't know if the air was the smell of death or of just not much living.

The first person I saw was Dale Porter, the chief of police. He was a friend and a member of my congregation.

"Morning, preacher," he said, almost in a whisper, the way people tend to talk around the dead.

"Hey, Dale. Is Mrs. McKinley still here?"

He shook his head. "They've already taken her to the funeral home. Robert has gone over there, too. I don't know where the kids are. They were here a few minutes ago."

Robert was Love McKinley's husband. He was one of the town's two lawyers and was active in county politics.

"I'll go find the children. I don't know what I'll say to them, though."

He put his hand on my arm.

"Before you go, I want to give you this. I found it in her room, lying on top of the Bible. The Bible was open."

"Should you be giving this to me?"

"This isn't a crime scene. And your name's on it, along with three or four others. And since it was on the Bible, I thought maybe you would have the best chance of figuring out if it was important."

I took the small slip of paper from him. It had four names on it, written in Love's boarding school script. Mine was the third one down. Her husband's was first, Dr. Winston's was second. The last name on the list was Leola Townsend's. There wasn't an obvious connection between any of them, except they all lived in Cleland.

"Do you know where the Bible was open to?" I asked. I didn't know whether it would make a difference or not, but it was the only thing I could think of.

"I don't know. Somewhere near the front. When I went back to look, somebody had closed it and put it on the bedside table."

"You're sure it's suicide and not an accidental overdose?"

"She took every pill in the bottle, and the date on the label was two days ago. Hard to take that many pills by accident."

I got back home about two hours later. I had talked to the son and the daughter, finding nothing to say except that I was sorry for their loss, unable to use any of the other trite phrases that I had in my bag. The fact that she committed suicide left too many questions and probably too many guilty feelings. Both the children looked stunned. I told them I would come back to see their father. Neither of them answered me.

Beth was in the kitchen when I got there. She spent a lot of her time there, baking cakes and pies and other sweets. The house almost always smelled like something was cooking or had just cooked. And I often found the cake, the pies, or a pan of cookies in the trash. I'd asked Beth why she'd thrown something that looked perfectly good to me in the trashcan. She just said, "It wasn't right."

I gave her a kiss on the cheek, looked to see what she was baking this time, and started toward my study.

"Did she really kill herself," Beth asked.

"Looks like it."

"I can understand that," Beth said. She never turned toward me.

I went into my study and sat down. One wall of the study was all the books I had accumulated at the seminary, and a few I had bought since then. I had read most of them. Another bookcase held books that I had bought recently, mostly philosophy and a few pop-science books. There was also a book that attempted to explain Buddhism.

I took the list of names out of my shirt pocket and stared at it. I was the third name on the list. I remembered that Love had come to see me two days ago. I didn't know her well. She came to church most Sundays but didn't participate in Sunday School or any of the Ladies groups. She, like a lot of others in my congregation, was sort of a ghostly presence on Sunday morning, staring at me in the pulpit and not to be seen again until a Sunday or several Sundays later. In my two years at Cleland Baptist Church, I'd gotten to know maybe thirty people well, another forty or fifty enough to immediately come up with their names and something about their lives. The rest, maybe four hundred, were on the rolls, sometimes in the pews, but not involved.

Too often, I had to perform funeral services for people I had never seen alive.

I tried to remember Love's visit. It was in the morning. I had gotten a late start because I had to make a sick visit at the hospital in Fortsburg. The drive there, a few minutes with the wife of one of the deacons, and the drive back took up a big part of the morning. When I got back to the church, Love was sitting there.

"Do you have a minute, pastor?" Her voice was soft, and there was some hesitancy as if she expected me to say I didn't have a minute.

I assured her that I did, and we went into the office.

When I sat down, I saw a stack of phone messages. Evidently, Gloria, the church secretary, was either on an errand or had taken an early lunch. Love sat down across the desk from me. She was dressed rather formally for a Tuesday in Cleland. She had on a light blue suit with a cream blouse that had a big collar. There was a jeweled brooch on the jacket. The suit looked expensive. It also looked like it had been bought twenty years ago.

I waited for her to tell me what she wanted, but she didn't say anything. I glanced at the stack of phone messages and decided I better get something moving.

"What did you want to see me for, Mrs. McKinley," I asked. I noticed that she had a handkerchief in her hands, and her fingers were twisting it. She was looking at the handkerchief.

"Let me rephrase that," I said. "What can I do for you?"

Finally, she looked up at me and said, "I wonder if God loves me."

I had been expecting something about her marriage or maybe her relationship with somebody else. But a question about her relationship with God, not in the abstract, but personal, took me by surprise.

"I'm certain that God loves you, just as he loves me. We're assured of that. But, could you tell me what makes you ask that?"

"I just need to know," she said. "Sometimes, I don't feel like God—or anybody else—loves me."

I started writing some scripture references on my notepad, starting with John 3:16 and ending with Luke 6:38. There were a half-dozen references to how God loves us. I hoped that would convince her.

I asked her to read these in her Bible and think about all that God had done for her and her family. And to know that the congregation—God's people—loved her. She took the paper and looked at it. Then she looked at me. Remembering it now, I think the look was asking if I had anything else, but I didn't see that at the time.

She thanked me and left.

That was, as best I could remember, the second time I had had any sort of conversation with her. Now, knowing what happened two days later, I could see that she was coming to me, hoping that I would help her out of the emotional hole she was in. I had given her a prescription for a half-dozen Bible verses and let her leave. I returned all my phone calls.

I went back into the kitchen. Beth was putting a cake on the table. It had chocolate icing.

"That looks good," I said.

"I hope it tastes good. What do you want for dinner tonight?"

"We still have some of that barbecue, don't we? Let's have that."

She nodded and continued to clean up the kitchen. I walked next door to the church.

In a couple of days, I would have to conduct Love's funeral. As Baptists, we don't have the same strictures on the burial of suicides that some denominations do. I wouldn't mention that she had decided she didn't want to live anymore, nor would I speculate on what on this side was so painful that the unknown on the other side was more tempting. I'd say she was a good woman, gone before her time, and everybody in the congregation would know that I was simply mouthing words. I had once thought I would be worth more. Now I sometimes wonder if I'm worth even that.

Instead of going into the church, I kept walking, heading downtown. Dr. Winston's clinic was on a side street just off Main. It was only a couple of blocks away. When I got there, one person was in the waiting room, and Mattie Kingry was at her desk behind the window. Mattie was the wife of Jim Kingry, one of our deacons.

"Hi, pastor. You sick or something."

Mattie was one of those people who always had a smile in her voice if not on her face. She was as close to a perpetually happy person as I've ever seen.

"Or something," I said. "I just need to see the doc for a few minutes."

"Sure. May have to wait 10 or 15 minutes. Clancy there's ahead of you, but the doc will make quick work of him, won't he, Clancy."

The man sitting in the corner looked up from the magazine. "Always does," he said and went back to his magazine.

It wasn't more than 10 minutes before Clancy came out, and Mattie told me to go on back.

Eric Winston and I were about the same age, and we had been in Cleland about the same length of time. He'd probably seen more of Cleland's citizens than I had, but I imagined he remembered fewer names. Everybody knew that he would probably be leaving in a few years; he was serving out some sort of contract that had helped him pay for medical school.

When I got to his office, Eric was typing some notes into his computer. His office was neat. A few papers stacked on his desk and some folders with patient names on labels across the top. Eric was lean, only about five foot eight, and looked like he'd always been in an office of some sort. I could imagine what the farmers thought when he touched them with his uncalloused hands.

He finished typing and turned to me.

"What brings you in this morning? Mattie says you're not sick."

"Right. I want to ask you about Love McKinley."

"What about her? I heard she committed suicide."

I pulled the notepaper out of my pocket and put it on his desk.

"She did. But before she did, she made this list. My name's on it. So's yours. She came to see me, and I wondered if she came to see you."

He picked up the list, looked at it, and handed it back to me.

"She did. And I guess that's about all I can tell you. HIPPA rules."

"She's dead. It won't hurt her, and it may help me help the family. Right now, I don't know what to do or say."

Eric shoved some papers around on his desk, picked up one, and stared at it. Then he put it down, his mouth clenched in a tight line, and shrugged.

"HIPPA says medical records are private for 50 years after the patient's death."

I started to say something, but he put up his hand.

"But," he said, "let me tell you a story."

I leaned back in my chair, waiting.

"Say that there's this small-town doctor. Really nice guy. And he had a bunch of patients he'd inherited from the doctor who had been treating them for the last thirty years. Some of the treatments weren't, so far as this small-town doctor was concerned, the best for the patient, but it might be better just to continue them than try to change them."

"What kind of treatments?" I asked.

"Oh, you know, different kinds. Bad diets. Bed rest instead of exercise." He stopped and looked straight at me. "Pain pills."

I nodded, and he went on.

"Now, say that one of the patients came to the doctor and said that he or she wanted to change the treatment. This treatment is something she's been doing for years. But she thinks it's important to change it. And the doctor considers the patient's age, general health, and—God help me—what he'd have to do to change the treatment. And he just writes him or her another prescription."

"Is that what happened with Love McKinley?"

"It's a story. Could have happened."

There was a sadness in the way he said it.

I waved to Mattie as I left the office. Obviously, Love was trying to make some changes in her life and get some questions answered. But the two visits I knew about weren't really alike. I'd heard rumors about her drug use. I'd also heard that she drank a lot. But, so far as I knew, I'd never seen her either drunk or stoned. The times I had seen her, she was so quiet she was almost not there. I figured that silence was the cost of living with somebody as blustery as Robert McKinley, but maybe there was something much deeper behind it.

When I got back to the church, there was a phone message from Alisha McKinley, Love and Robert's daughter. I dialed her back. She wanted to make an appointment for the family to talk about the funeral arrangements. They had already decided to have the service at the funeral home instead of the church, but they wanted me to officiate. I told her I'd be glad to. She thanked me, and we set a time to meet the next morning.

"Alisha, before you go, could you tell me something about your mother? I didn't know her very well, and I want to make the service meaningful for those who did know her."

There was a silence; then, what sounded like a quiet sob.

"Not many people knew her. She's been alone ever since she came to Cleland, except for Dad, Bob, and me. I think that might have been part of the problem."

"The problem?"

"When we were young, she seemed to be happy. She took us places, and she played the piano. She played the piano very well. Sang, too. Then we went off to college, and when I came home, I noticed she didn't seem as happy. I asked Dad about it. He just said that when people get older they change. But she didn't play the piano anymore. I never heard her sing."

I made a note about the piano and singing. I didn't write down that she was unhappy and lonely.

That night Beth and I sat in the living room, her on the sofa and me in my recliner, staring at the television. There was some sort of procedural cop show on, but I wasn't keeping up with it. I was thinking about what I had learned about Love McKinley.

"Where have you gone?"

It took me a minute to register that Beth was talking to me. I turned, and she was looking at me. A tear in the corner of her eye.

"What?"

"Where have you gone?"

"What do you mean. I'm right here. I haven't gone anywhere?"

"I don't mean physically. I mean emotionally. You come home. We exchange a couple of sentences. You leave again. Then you come home, and we exchange a couple more sentences."

"I don't know what you're getting at."

"I mean that we don't know each other anymore. That we talk like a couple of acquaintances who meet on the street. That what we used to have that kept us together when things were hard has disappeared."

"What do you mean, we don't know each other. We've been married almost ten years. How can you be married ten years and not know somebody?"

The tear rolled down her cheek. She wiped it away.

"Do you know that I spent part of this afternoon lying on the bed, crying, praying that I could die?"

I felt a wave of dizziness.

We tried to talk, but our words kept running into the same walls of sadness that couldn't be defined. Another piece of the world that I thought I knew had crumbled, and all I could see were the pieces. I'd ask her why she was so sad, and her response was that she didn't know. She just was. I had had three courses in pastoral counseling, but none said what I should do when my wife told me she wanted to die.

Finally, we just gave up. Beth got up, gave me a light kiss on the cheek, and wandered into the bedroom, leaving me to wonder what I should do. I loved Beth. I still wanted to spend the rest of my life with her. I was faithful to every vow that we'd made when we were married. But she didn't see much happiness in her future.

And what I hadn't told her was that I didn't either. As a husband. As a pastor. Or even as a human being.

I went to my study and got a modern translation of the Bible. Dale had said that the Bible had been opened to a place near the front, maybe Genesis. So, I started reading at the very first page. After an hour, I was up to Noah. I stopped to examine every story, looking for some clue. Maybe the list had just been laid on the Bible and didn't mean anything. But, maybe it did, and since I was connected by having my name on it, I wanted to know.

I wanted to know what I could do to help Beth.

I wanted to know if I could have helped Love.

But I was tired, and it was too late to do anything. So, I went to bed. Beth was already asleep or pretending to be. In about a half-hour, I was, too.

The next morning, we sat at the table with our coffee. I asked her how she was feeling, and she said, "Fine."

"Can you tell me more than that about how you're feeling?" I said. "I worry about your lying on the bed crying."

"Don't worry about it. I was just feeling down." She got up to pour herself another cup of coffee.

"Do you feel down often?"

"Sometimes. But I'll get over it." Then she took her coffee and left the room, leaving me wondering why she had said, "I will get over it" instead of "I've gotten over it."

As I sipped my coffee, it occurred to me that our conversations were like that more often than not, raising questions rather than giving information. I tried to remember when we last had a real conversation. I tried to remember when there was any intimacy in what we talked about. It seemed like everything just skated on the surface.

That had seemed comfortable. I was feeling like I was dealing with everything I could; so, when she said she was fine, it was easy to believe her despite the evidence of my own eyes. I finished my coffee and walked next door to the church.

Robert McKinley and his children were due at 10:30 to discuss the funeral, and they were prompt; at 10:30, Robert, Alisha, and Bobby were shown into my office. Alisha's eyes were swollen and red; she looked like she was at the end of a long, sad march. Bobby was quiet and somber. The only person who looked out of place was Robert. He didn't seem so sad as distracted, as if this was one more meeting he didn't want to have.

We spent a few minutes sketching out the service. I suggested that perhaps members of the choir could provide some music. I asked whether they had anyone else they wanted to deliver the eulogy or maybe say a few words. They didn't. They wanted the service to be at the funeral home. Robert said that the funeral director had suggested an eleven o'clock funeral with visitation the night before.

When I asked if there was anything they would particularly like to mention in the service, Bobby spoke first.

"She was a good mom. I know she had her problems, but she was a good mom."

Alisha's head snapped toward him. "Did you ever tell her that?"

Bobby didn't answer. He just looked down at his hands.

"Look, pastor," Alisha said. "I know that my mother was an unhappy person at the end of her life. I mean, she committed suicide just to get out of it. But she wasn't always like that. She was a good mom when we needed her, and that's what I'd like for anybody who wants to come to the funeral to know."

I looked at Robert to see if he had anything to add, but he was looking in the other direction.

We talked for a few more minutes, and I told them that I thought I had all that I needed. Love and her family had been members of the church for years, and certainly, I would mention that. I'd read Proverbs 31 and John 14. Some members of the choir would sing "It Is Well with My Soul," and we'd just have a prayer at the interment. It would be a simple service, but it would honor the memory of Love. The family seemed satisfied, and I knew it would be sufficient. I had done this same service a half-dozen times in the last two years.

As they were leaving, I asked Robert if I could have a few words with him. He hesitated, but Alisha told him that they could walk home, and they would see him there. Robert nodded and came back into the office. He sat back down in the chair he'd just left.

I pulled the list out of my pocket and handed it to him.

"Does this mean anything to you?"

He studied it for a minute.

"Where did this come from? It's Love's handwriting. My name's on it. Yours too. The doctor's. And Leola's."

"It was in Love's bedroom when Dale got there."

"But why'd he give it to you? Why didn't he give it to me?"

"I don't know. Maybe because it was on top of an open Bible. You can keep it if you want to."

Robert dropped the list back on my desk.

"No. It doesn't mean anything to me. There's no reason I'd want to keep it."

He started to get up, and I held up my hand.

"Can you give me just a couple more minutes? I'm still trying to puzzle this out."

He nodded and leaned back in his chair.

"I've talked to Eric, and he said that Love had been to see him. He wouldn't tell me what they talked about—doctor-patient confidentiality, but I know from her meeting with me she was looking for some sort of change in her life, some sort of assurance. Do you know what she may have been looking for from the doctor?"

I thought I saw something in Robert's eyes, but he turned his head. When he turned back to face me, he had the same distracted expression.

"I don't know," he said. "I suppose you're aware that she had a problem with pain pills. She's been taking them for years. When the new doctor came, he just kept prescribing them because the other doctor had. Maybe she just needed another prescription."

I didn't mention that the new prescription, the one with the pills that had killed Love, had been filled the day before she saw Eric.

"How about conversations with you? Did anything seem different?"

"We didn't talk much," he said. He looked down at his hands, hiding his eyes from me. "We quit talking a long time ago. Mostly we just lived apart in the same house."

He stopped, looking around the room, trying to find something to fix his eyes on. Then he looked again at his hands.

"She did do something unusual," he said. "Yesterday, when I came down to fix my breakfast, she was already up and had made the coffee. She didn't usually get up before I left for the office."

"Do you mind telling me what you talked about?"

He shook his head. "Not much. She said something about a dance we went to in college, some sorority thing. I didn't remember it."

"Anything else?"

"No. I think she said something about maybe a vacation, but I don't remember. We haven't done anything like that in ten years or more. I left and went to the office."

He got up.

"I appreciate what you're trying to do, pastor, but I think you're just wasting your time. Love was in a lot of pain. More emotional pain than anything else. And she quit being the woman I married a long time ago. I can't help but think that she's better off now, and I can't be sorry that she's not in pain anymore."

He turned and walked out of my office.

After he left, I wondered if he wasn't right. I believed that there were a lot of things worse than death, and going day to day in a pain that crippled your ability to live a fulfilling life could well be one of them. I thought about Beth. What was the difference between Love and Beth? Was it that Beth just didn't have the means at hand? Or was it that she hadn't completely given up on her life? At least not yet.

I felt the tears running down my cheeks. Then I wondered just how different I was from Robert McKinley.

Since I was sixteen, I had felt that I had a course set for my life. I had walked down the aisle of that little Baptist Church and announced that I had been called to the ministry and that I was going to devote the rest of my life to that. It was an evening service, and there probably weren't more than twenty people there. A couple of the older ladies came up to me after the service and said they would pray for me. One of them called me a "sky-pilot." She said that's what they used to call ministers.

Nothing in the rest of my high school years or even my college years changed that. I was active in the church. I didn't drink. I felt remorse for my impure thoughts. I read the Bible and even attempted to pull out some of the meanings that, to my young faith, didn't seem all that obvious. In college, I met Beth and immediately fell in love with her.

Beth was Christian but different from me. She didn't make a big deal of it; she lived it quietly. If there was someone she knew who needed help, Beth went to help, expecting neither reward nor thanks. I watched her and learned a lot about what really being a Christian was.

We married before I entered seminary, and between some financial help from my home church and a job as a youth minister in one of the larger churches in town, we managed to get by. We tried to make sure that Beth didn't get pregnant before I graduated.

I graduated from seminary and immediately accepted a call to be assistant pastor at a large church in North Carolina. I was embarrassed that I took so much pleasure in the fact that the salary was much larger than the offers that some of my classmates were getting. I told myself that the money didn't matter; it was the service. But being able to provide for Beth and the children we were going to have didn't hurt either.

We decided that it was time to start a family, and Beth got pregnant almost immediately. She blossomed. Always a happy person, she seemed to radiate that happiness to everybody around her, infecting them with the joy she was feeling.

Then, in the fifth month of her pregnancy, at a routine OB visit, the doctor couldn't hear the baby's heartbeat. After some more tests, he called us into his office and told us that the baby had died before being born.

We couldn't understand that. Beth was healthy. I was healthy. So far as we knew until that morning in the doctor's office, the baby was healthy. Then, suddenly, the baby was not.

The doctor assured us that this didn't mean that Beth couldn't have healthy children. He said that sometimes, the conditions were not right, and this was nature's way of preventing a severely deformed or nearly dead child from being born. In other words, something was wrong. I tried to tell myself that I should be thankful God had created a plan for us, that this was God's will, and that we'd have other children. I'm not sure I believed it, even as I told myself that it was true.

Beth did become pregnant again, but she miscarried much earlier. The doctors did all sorts of tests and couldn't find a reason that she shouldn't be able to carry a baby to term. They told us that we could have children. But Beth didn't believe them.

For her, the sorrow she felt at the loss of two children was all she could stand in this life; so, she refused to try again. I wanted children, but I didn't want Beth to suffer as she had. After ten years of marriage, we were childless, and the ghosts of those two unborn babies seemed to be very large between us.

I came home early that day, determined to see what I could do to help Beth, but she wasn't there. Her car was gone, and I guessed she was either shopping or at the grocery. I went into my study and picked up the Bible I had been reading. I was convinced that there was some connection between the note and something in the Bible. Something near the front of the Bible.

I had finished the part about Noah and the flood and was puzzling about whether it told me anything about Love when I heard the garage door. I put the Bible down and went to the back door just as Beth was coming in, carrying three shopping bags, all from the only locally-owned department store in town.

"Been shopping?" I asked before I could stop myself. I knew better than to ask questions with such obvious answers.

"Yes. I bought a few new clothes at the sale. Maybe perk up my mood."

I had heard of retail therapy, but I didn't have anything to say. I thought that any mood improvement would be temporary at best, but that sounded like I was blaming her. So, I just smiled and nodded. She took the bags into the bedroom.

I followed her and watched her put the bags on the bed.

"How are you feeling today?"

She glanced at me over her shoulder and continued taking her purchases out of the bag.

"Well, I'm not lying on the bed wishing I was dead, if that's what you mean. That's something."

I couldn't see her face, but there was a brittleness in the tone of her voice that made me wonder if that was really true. Once, not all that long ago, she would have come in, given me a kiss, and told me about her day shopping or dealing with the ladies of the congregation. Now she told me nothing. I didn't know whether this was because she was being reticent or simply because—from her view—there was simply nothing to tell.

I stood there a moment, looking at her back. She continued to empty bags, acting as if I weren't there. I began to agree with her.

I left and went into my study. It wasn't that I didn't have something to do. I needed to prepare for Love McKinley's funeral. There would still be a sermon Sunday. There were two books on my desk, one on Christian ethics and another on whether Christianity meant the same thing as following Jesus. But I sat there and did nothing, wondering why a large part of my life was in the next room, making her life a fortress of solitude.

Once, right after I had become the associate pastor, I had to deliver the Sunday sermon because the Senior Pastor was conducting a revival at another church. I remember Beth sitting in the second pew, beaming at me. I don't remember what I said, but I remember that she seemed proud that I was saying it.

After the service, she heard one of the women say something about my being so young. She smiled at the woman and nodded. "He'll get over it," she said. The ladies in the group all laughed. Before we left that church, I think the women loved her almost as much as I did.

I heard Beth in the kitchen, and I wanted to go out and make some sort of contact with her, talk to her, or put my arms around her and hold her. But I didn't. I didn't know how to break through the barrier that she had thrown up between us. So I knelt beside my desk and prayed. I stumbled because I didn't know what to pray for. Peace for Beth. For me to be a better husband. For me to find the reservoir of faith that seemed to have been leaking away over the past two or three years. For God to give us a child that would banish the ghosts of the two unborn children and pull us back together.

I couldn't decide. I didn't feel led. So, I just knelt beside my desk and silently screamed "Help!" to God.

Of all the people on Love McKinley's list, the one I most dreaded visiting was Leola Townsend. She was a Methodist, not a member of my congregation. And, for reasons I'd never been able to figure out, she was considered the grande dame of Cleland. Her family went back to the founding of the town, but that was true of most of Cleland's citizens. She was wealthy but no more than some others. The one thing I had noticed about Leola Townsend was her imperious air, as if she were an uncrowned empress.

When things were being decided around Cleland, her name would often come up, and her nod would usually settle a question. Just as the lack of it would sink it.

I called her from the church to ask if I might drop by. She didn't ask why I wanted to see her; I suppose she was used to holding audiences.

Leola Townsend's rambling two-story wooden house was one of the largest in Cleland and probably dated back to before the town was incorporated. Her father and her grandfather, both named Pender Roberts, had accumulated hundreds of acres of land and owned several stores on Main Street. I knew that because Leola Townsend was often a topic of conversation among the townspeople.

To an outsider, there seemed to be two Leola Townsends. One was the woman who lived in the big house on Main Street and seemed to have more influence than anyone could give me a reason for. The other was the one that was talked about wherever the church women gathered with a mixture of romantic awe and pity. Fred Townsend had come to Cleland from somewhere down on the coast to work for Pender Roberts, Jr. some sixty years ago. From the gossip, I gathered that Townsend was young, well-educated, and very handsome. The young Leola Roberts fell in love with him, her father approved, and they were married in a storied wedding with more bride's maids and ushers than Cleland had ever seen. Pender Roberts built them a house further up Main Street, and the young couple seemed to have started on a charmed life.

But—and here the story varies according to who's telling it—Fred Townsend either got involved with another woman and left, or after two years of being married to Leola, he decided that the family wealth wasn't worth having to live with her. She'd been a bride at twenty and abandoned at twenty-two.

It was said that Leola begged her dad to send some men to find Fred and bring him back, but Pender Roberts, Jr. had refused. He had said that no man who would leave the family was good enough to return to it. And that is how it had been these last sixty years. She'd sold the house her father built her and moved back into the family mansion.

It was an interesting story, full of disappointed love, money, and bits and pieces of stories of Leola compensating for her abandonment by becoming the closest thing Cleland had to a society doyen. The only first-hand knowledge I had of the story was when I called on her as a part of a religious census the church was conducting. For some reason, probably because the house she lived in was usually called the Roberts House, I wrote Leola Roberts on the census card. She angrily informed me that her name was Leola Townsend or Mrs. Fred Townsend. I had quickly changed it.

From the street, the Roberts House looked exactly like you would expect: large, well-kept, a testament to old money in a relatively young town. But as I walked up the sidewalk, I noticed that paint was peeling on the large porch columns and that several of the boards on the porch were warping up. The brick steps leading up to the porch had a large crack running down them.

I knocked on the door, and it was answered by Mrs. Townsend's maid, a Black woman in a black dress and white apron. She was probably as old as Mrs. Townsend. I told her who I was and that I had an appointment with Mrs. Townsend.

She nodded and led me back to a large, dark sitting room. The heavy beige draperies were closed, and the room had a cave-like closeness. Leola Townsend was sitting in a wingback chair in a circle of light thrown by a floor lamp, reading. When the maid motioned me in, Mrs. Townsend looked up, her puzzled expression telling me that she didn't know who I was or why I was there. Then, she remembered our appointment. As if someone had thrown a switch, she smiled and laid her book on the side table.

"I was wondering what I owed the pleasure of this visit, pastor. Even my own pastor doesn't come here often." There was a playfulness in her tone that I didn't expect from her. It didn't seem appropriate to either her age or her position. She motioned me to the chair on the other side of the table.

I sat down, trying to decide how I was going to broach the subject. Finally, I decided I had nothing to lose by being direct.

"I'm trying to solve something of a mystery," I said. "It has to do with Love McKinley."

"Yes, I heard that she committed suicide. Terrible thing. But I don't know how I can help you. I hardly knew Mrs. McKinley."

"She didn't leave a suicide note, but she did leave some sort of note. It had four names on it. Mine was on it. So was yours. Love McKinley came to see me the day before she died. I wondered if she came to see you."

Leola Townsend looked at the window. There was no view; the drapery was closed. I had the feeling that she just wanted to look somewhere else, not at me. She didn't answer. I just waited. Finally, she turned back to me.

"We probably could have been friends," she said, slowly, thoughtfully. "I'm told she came from a good family. Her husband was a professional man. But there was something about her when she came to Cleland, something that made it seem like she wanted everything immediately. She was young, and I suppose I should have recognized it as some sort of youthful exuberance. But I found it off-putting, just as my friends did."

I nodded. I didn't know what to make of this, but it was the first thing that had come to Mrs. Townsend's mind, instead of just answering my question. I did what I had been taught in Pastoral Counseling, just nodding to show I accepted the statement and waiting for the next one.

"Yes, she did come to see me. I suppose it was the same day she went to see you."

I nodded again, but there seemed to be no next statement coming from her. I decided that that was as much as she was going to volunteer, so I asked her what they had talked about.

"I'm sure I don't remember," she said. "It was a very brief visit. I don't know why she thought she had to see me."

"But, did anything stand out. Catch your attention?"

She made a little, annoyed sound. I didn't know if she was annoyed at my questions or at the memory that the question had prompted.

"Would you like a glass of iced tea?" she asked. Then without waiting for my answer, she summoned the Black woman and asked her to get us some tea. "I hope you like it sweet," she said.

We sat in silence for a moment, listening to the clinking of glasses and the opening and closing of the refrigerator door. Once the tea was in our hands, Mrs. Townsend leaned back in her chair, staring at the drops of condensation on her glass.

"I suppose it serves no purpose to protect either Mrs. McKinley or me," she said. "Yes, I remember what was said. I remember what she said. And I remember how I felt when she said it. She said she wanted to make some changes, and part of those changes needed my help."

"How was that?"

"She said something about living in solitary confinement for too long. She wanted to be someone who enjoyed things, looked forward to things. I told her I could understand that. Then she asked for my help. And I told her I didn't know how I could help her. Mostly I sit here nearly in the dark. Mabel cooks and cleans the two or three rooms I use in this old barn. Once I had a circle of friends, but many of them are dead, several are in nursing homes, and nobody visits me, and I don't visit anyone. I told her that she had essentially come to the cemetery looking for life. It wasn't here."

"What did she say?"

"Nothing really. She began to cry. She sat in that chair, where you're sitting, and she looked at me and cried.

"What happened then?"

"Nothing. She cried. Then she quit crying, pulled herself together. She thanked me for seeing her and left. She didn't wait for Mable to show her out. It seemed like she was just ready to leave. I don't know how she expected me to help her."

I couldn't think of anything else to ask Mrs. Townsend. Just as Love had, I thanked her for seeing me, and I left. I heard her call Mable to see me out, but I was already out the front door before Mable appeared. I had evidently been there longer than I had thought because when I stepped out onto the broad porch, the dusk outside almost matched the darkness inside. The days were getting shorter in Cleland. For some, like Love, they had shortened to nothing. I decided not to stop by the church, but to go straight home. There was nothing I could do at the church this late.

Then it occurred to me that there was probably nothing I could do at home either.

When I got to the corner, just before I turned to go one block over to the parsonage, I stopped and pulled the list from my pocket. There were four names. There were four conversations. And evidently, Love didn't find in any of them what she was looking for. In one or more of those four conversations, somebody had a chance to do something different, to provide her with an answer that might have prevented her from taking her own life. But we didn't. She didn't.

The easy answer was that Love McKinley was a deeply troubled woman who had blunted her troubles with alcohol and pain killers for a lot of years and finally had simply given up. But my mind wouldn't accept the easy answer; she could have done that in her bedroom without involving four other people. It was almost as if we were some sort of test as to whether her life was worth living. And we had all failed the test.

When I got home, Beth was in the living room. The television was on, but I couldn't tell what she was watching or if she was watching. She was sitting in the wingback chair, stiffly erect, both feet on the floor. There was no sign of relaxation or repose. She just sat there, a mannequin in a wingback chair. I leaned over and kissed her on the cheek and felt no reaction. Then she turned her head to me and nodded.

"I guess I better get dinner started," she said. She stood up and went into the kitchen. I watched as she walked, a little stiff-legged as if she had been sitting there, upright with her feet on the floor, for a long time.

When we were dating, I could usually tell what Beth's mood was from her eyes. She was one of those people whose eyes are far more expressive than their mouth. When she was happy, they sparkled. And when she was angry, which wasn't often, it was as if sparks were shooting out while her eyes bored holes in you.

That was the biggest difference. Not the stiffness or the posture. But the eyes. Eyes that were like the windows of a house that was dark and empty.

I started to go into the kitchen, but that felt like stalking. She had got up to leave me. I needed to honor that. Or maybe I was just afraid of what I'd find if I went in there. So, I went to my study and picked up the Bible. I opened it the chapter in Genesis where I had left off. Chapter 15. Where Abraham makes Hagar pregnant. When Hagar became pregnant, the Bible said that she despised Sarah, Abraham's wife.

I stopped there and thought about it. Although it was Sarah's idea for Abraham to have a child by Hagar, it wasn't working out, and Sarah gave Abraham an ultimatum: it's her or me. Abraham told her to do what she needed to do, and Sarah mistreated Hagar. Hagar ran away. And an angel visited her.

This passage was full of conflict and strife. Maybe that's what Love was feeling. Maybe she was running away from this life.

But that didn't make sense. Neither did Chapter 17, where God told Abraham that every male should be circumcised. I was still thinking about that when Beth tapped on my study door.

"Would you like some dinner?" she asked. Her voice was almost normal, soft without the bitter edge I had noticed the day before. "I made some pasta and a salad."

I put the Bible down, and we went into the kitchen. Beth had asked me about my seeing Leola Townsend, and I told her about my visit to the cave-like room. We were having a real conversation, except that it didn't say what either of us was feeling. Mostly we ate in silence. Then she began to clear the table, and I went back to my study.

There was a time when the end of the day was our favorite time. We had done things, and we shared those things. We would weave our individual activities into a single strand in the evening. Then I couldn't imagine a day without Beth or a night when she wouldn't help me make some sense of what had happened that day.

I had learned quickly enough that being a minister wasn't exactly as I had envisioned it. The pastors in my home church were people who stood at a distance, figures in the pulpit looking down on those of us in the seats. I didn't know about the calls at night. Or sitting beside a wife or husband in the hospital. I didn't know about what a twenty-something seminary graduate had to do to make sense of the pain a seventy-year-old man was going through as he watched his wife slowly die. Or worse, continue to live but forget him and their children.

I hadn't had a call like that in a while, but every time the phone rang, I expected it to be someone trying to talk through tears. Now I felt like I needed to call someone. But there was no one to call.

I picked up a book, stared at the pages for a few minutes, then put it back down. I had this nagging feeling that what I needed wasn't outside of me, but inside. It wasn't something I could find in a book or even if I found someone to call. I had prayed. The Bible said to pray without ceasing. For a while, I had. Then I didn't. I still believed that God was there. I just wasn't sure He wanted anything to do with me.

Finally, I gave up and went to bed. Beth was breathing softly, her body as near the edge of the bed as she could get, making sure that, even when she was asleep, I wasn't going to get too close. I was thinking about what that meant when I finally drifted off to sleep.

The entire town turned out for Love McKinley's funeral. People who never visited her or wouldn't even greet her on the street came. The funeral home chapel wasn't large, and it was full, with twenty or thirty people standing along the back wall. While the choir was singing, I studied the faces in front of me and wondered if one of them had what Love had been looking for on her last day on this earth. Obviously, she was looking for something. And just as obviously, she hadn't found it.

The one face I looked for and couldn't find was Leola Townsend. She was true to her own opinions to the very end.

The choir finished, and I went to the lectern at the front of the chapel. I had prepared my notes, and I planned to say everything Alisha and Bobby asked me to say. I talked about her family and how she was a good mother to her children. I talked about her talents. I talked about the vivacious person she was when she was raising a family.

The people in the congregation kept their eyes fixed on me, appearing to believe what I was saying, appearing to ignore the large unasked question behind it all: what was in Love McKinley's mind when she went into her bedroom, sat down with a bottle of pills and her Bible, laid the Bible down and took the pills?

My eulogy didn't take more than about 10 minutes, but it seemed much too long. I was saying very little but using a lot of words. Alisha sat on the front pew, tears running down her cheeks. Bobby took her hand. Robert just sat there, staring straight ahead. Maybe it was, as he had said, better that Love had ended her life, and with it, had ended her pain. Maybe Robert was right after all.

After the service, the funeral director and his people, all in dark suits and white shirts, rolled the casket up the aisle and moved it to the back of the hearse. There were no pallbearers. Just Love and several relative strangers. The symmetry of her life and death struck me as ironic. The family got into the first car behind the hearse, and I went to mine. A few of the cars fell in behind us as we left the church parking lot for the short drive to the cemetery.

At the cemetery, I said a short prayer. A few people spoke to the family. And everybody wandered off. I stood back from the grave watching. Within minutes there was no one left but Alisha and Bobby, standing beside the grave staring at the casket. Again, Bobby reached over and took Alisha's hand. I don't know why, but it occurred to me that neither of them had mentioned being married or having been married. It appeared that the McKinley line was about to end with these two, standing shoulder to shoulder, holding hands, and staring into their mother's grave.

I stood quietly until they turned and started walking back to the family car. Then I went to the edge of the grave. I probably looked like I was praying, but I wasn't. I was apologizing. I knew that I—and Lord knows how many others—had failed Love. And this was the result of that failure.

I went back to the church after the funeral and piddled around with administrative tasks, mostly reading committee reports. For a small church, ours had a lot of committees. The only ones I especially paid attention to were those that could make a dent in the church budget, like Buildings and Grounds. The rest I scanned and threw in the outbox to be filed. Most of the church records had been digitized, including the committee reports, but the deacons still wanted paper copies in metal file cabinets.

Turning to the computer, I looked up Love McKinley's membership record. It was sparse. It showed that she had joined the church nearly forty years ago, but there were just a couple of notes on the record. One was when the Benevolence committee visited her with flowers after her mother's death. The other one was when two of the deacons visited her in the hospital. That was ten years ago. There were no notes of pastoral visits, but I didn't know whether that was because the pastor hadn't made a note on her card or whether he had never visited her. I knew I hadn't.

The nearly blank record fit neatly with the lonely life Love seemed to have led. It occurred to me that I had never met her children until this week. If they visited her, they didn't come to church together.

I closed the church administration program, knowing that I knew nothing more and that to continue was futile. This was, I thought, the time to tend to the living.

Beth was watching the news when I got home. I sat down beside her on the sofa.

"Any good news tonight?" I asked.

"Nope.

We sat there quietly, the television screen changing the light in the room as the news moved from story to story.

There had been another shooting, but they didn't know who did it. A limousine carrying women to a wedding party had crashed head-on into a semi. All the women were killed. A state official was being investigated for accepting bribes.

Beth was right. There was no good news.

"What you think about me leaving the ministry?" I asked. The words were out of my mouth before I even knew what I was saying. I hadn't thought about giving up my pastorate. Now I was asking my wife what she thought about the idea.

She looked at me. There didn't seem to be a lot of surprise in her expression. She looked back at the television, then clicked it off.

"I wondered if you were thinking about that," she said. She was still staring at the blank TV screen.

"I didn't know I was."

"I don't think that that's what's wrong with us," she said.

"Maybe it's what's wrong with me. I don't know what I'm doing here."

"Here?"

"In this church. In this town. In this job. Maybe, even in this marriage. I feel lost."

She turned to face me, her expression telling me nothing.

"Now, you know how I feel."

She got up to go to the kitchen, leaving me sitting there. I don't know what I had hoped for when I told Beth that I was thinking of giving up the ministry, but I was certain that it was more than that. That we were both lost, perhaps hopeless. I heard her pulling pans out of the cabinet, making one more meal.

I went into my study and picked up my Bible. I seemed to be collecting people who were lost. Love, lost and taking her life. I imagine that Robert was, in his way, lost too. He had married a woman who slowly but certainly changed to someone else. He seemed to have changed by not caring anymore. Beth. Me. Who knows who else? Wandering around in the world without going anywhere.

I turned on the lamp beside my chair. There was a soft pool of light, but beyond its edges, the room was getting darker and darker.

I opened the Bible to the place I had stopped earlier. Still in Genesis. I got to Chapter 18, where Abraham received the angels and told him that Sarah would have a child. Sarah laughs. Then she says she didn't laugh. But she did.

I remembered my seminary professor talking about how hard it is for us to believe in concrete miracles. We believe in them in the abstract. But not for us. Sarah couldn't believe that somebody as old as she was, somebody who had never had a child, could get pregnant. It was laughable.

And the angel didn't scold her. All he said was, "Yes, you did laugh."

Maybe God expected us to be weak, not to have much faith. I thought about how, Sunday by Sunday, I thought of myself more as an imposter, saying things that I couldn't live. It would be nice to know if that's what God expected from me, nothing better. I know I expected more.

Then I read Abraham's negotiation with the angels, trying to save Lot by saving Sodom.

He bargained the Lord down from fifty to ten. "For the sake of ten, I will not destroy it," the Lord said.

I couldn't remember what the population of Sodom was supposed to be, but ten people couldn't have been a big part of it. If the Lord could have found just that many, Sodom would have been spared. But it wasn't. I started to read on, but something held me up. There was something about Abraham's negotiation that seemed important.

Love's list.

Was this her negotiation with herself, what she required to keep from destroying Love McKinley?

I wondered how her negotiation went. First, she needed four people, then three, then two. Somehow, I thought that she negotiated herself all the way down to one. If she found even one person who cared, it would be reason enough to live.

I was still thinking about it when I saw Beth standing in the doorway. Her cheeks were wet where trails of tears were still unwiped.

"I don't want you to leave the ministry," she said.

I shook my head. "I don't know if I want to. I just know that I don't want to keep going like I am now."

She crossed over to me, her face becoming brighter as she entered the circle of light cast by the lamp. She knelt beside my chair.

"I failed Love McKinley," I said. "I think that all she needed was one person who cared. She wanted to rescue her own life, but she needed some help. Nobody helped her."

I realized as I said it that I was crying. No, I was sobbing. I was awash in my own guilt for passing Love McKinley off with a couple of Bible verses. Beth reached up and put her arms around my shoulders, and I slipped out of my chair, down on my knees beside her.

Beth put her face into my shoulder, and I could feel her tears wetting my shirt.

"I'm sorry," she said. "I'm sorry you had to face that. And I'm sorry that I was so into my own misery that I couldn't see what you were facing."

I pulled back and looked at her.

"You don't have anything to be sorry about," I said.

She shook her head.

"I have more to be sorry about than you know. There were the days that I thought about how easy it would be to just be dead. And there were other days that I thought that if I left you, all the pain would be gone. And then there were days when I didn't know what to do but scream."

Finally, we both just sat down on the floor, and I held Beth's hand. We were both still crying.

"What can I do to help you?" I said.

"I don't know. Maybe you already have. I thought I was all alone in this, but maybe both of us being broken makes us stronger."

I got up and went to my bookshelves. I found the book I was looking for and flipped it open to the front.

"The world breaks everyone, and afterward, many are strong in the broken places. But those that will not break it kills." I read her the quote and put the book back on the shelf.

"Who was that?" she asked.

"Ernest Hemingway."

She nodded. "Theology and tequila."

Then she laughed. It's the first real laugh I had heard from her in weeks. I started laughing, too, and in a moment, we were in a tangle on the floor, laughing as the pent-up tension poured out of us. When we stopped laughing, we just lay there, holding each other.

It was a strange evening. Tears. Laughter. Love. And at the end of it, nothing outside of ourselves had changed. Love McKinley was still in her grave. All of us on the list had still failed her. And I couldn't see how I should have felt lighter or better. But something had changed in me. We spent hours that evening talking. Talking about never being able to have children. About never being able to meet all of the standards we set for ourselves. About dealing with our own humanness.

It was nearly three in the morning before we got up from the floor and trudged into the bedroom. We hadn't had dinner; it was still partly prepared in the kitchen. We fell onto the bed in each other's arm.

The next day I woke up before Beth and went into the kitchen to make coffee. While I watched the coffee trickle into the pot, I tried to make sense of what had happened. I didn't know how long this gap between us had been growing. Beth had said that she was so into her own misery that she didn't recognize mine. That must have gone both ways.

But there was a difference. I was able to hide mine longer. I had been better at constructing a façade that kept people from seeing inside. I suppose that somehow I had gone around looking capable and pious, going through the motions of being a pastor and a Christian. It was only when I allowed Beth to look inside that she saw that much of the outside was a mask, and the inside was a mess.

I had been taught all of my life to be Stoic, to absorb what came—either good or bad—and show little or no reaction. My father had been that way, and I imagine his father and his father's father. Stoicism was in our breeding. But, I realized now that the same thing that held the emotions in also held other people out. For Beth, it must have been like living with one of the figures on Easter Island.

I was praying that I could be both more open and accepting when I heard Beth shuffle into the kitchen, her slippers making little rasping sounds on the hardwood floors. She put her arms around me, holding me tightly. I held her. It felt like we weren't apart anymore.

Sunday morning, after the choir had sung "It Is Well with My Soul," I went to the pulpit. A couple of hundred pairs of eyes looked at me, expecting me to say something profound or comforting or at least understandable. Instead, I said, "Today, I feel like one of the men on the road to Emmaus."

Several of the eyes blinked.

"You know, the men who were walking along the dusty, dirty road talking about the tragedy that had just happened in Jerusalem. They were joined by a stranger, so they told him about the tragedy.

"They were really down, and probably everything they said to each other just made them feel worse because the Crucifixion was a tragedy beyond their understanding. They asked the stranger if he hadn't heard of it."

"They walked and talked for miles, feeling bad, feeling helpless. And they didn't recognize that the Christ they were mourning was walking right beside them.

"That's why I feel like I'm one of the men on the road to Emmaus. I've been walking along, trying to absorb the helplessness I felt, and, tragically, not providing the help that some of you needed because all I could see was the dusty road, and all I could feel was the loss. I didn't look up and see that walking right beside me was Christ.

"I had forgotten his promise to be with me always, even unto the end of the age."

Then I talked about the view that we saw when we had downcast eyes, just dirt and dust, but when we raised our eyes and looked around, there was the Christ, doing exactly what he said he would do. Then I referenced the choir anthem.

"And," I said, "that's when we can say it is well; it is well with my soul.

I looked at Beth in the second row of pews. She was smiling. She was nodding.

The King of the World

I was twelve years old when I learned that the King of the World lived in a chicken coop. The three of us—Li'l Fowler, Billy Royce and I—had roller skated down to the end of Church Street, and then, after carefully hiding our skates in the weeds, had walked down the dirt road to the power plant and taken the path that Li'l had shown us through the woods.

And there it was, just like Li'l had said it would be. An old, nearly falling down chicken coop with hens walking around it, pecking on the ground and an old rooster sitting in the doorway. It wasn't painted. It was just boards. But near the flat roof, over the door, in brown or what might have been red paint, it said, "Cursed be anybody who steals my eggs." It was signed, "The King of the World."

Trying to stay hidden in the weeds, we crawled as close as we could to the chicken coop. Li'l was looking pretty proud.

"I told you," he said. "This is where Ol' Hezekiah lives. He lives with the chickens."

"I ain't seen Hezekiah yet," Billy Royce said. "All I see is a bunch of chickens."

I didn't say anything. I was still reading the sign over the door. "Cursed be anybody who steals my eggs. The King of the World." I was wondering what kind of curse. And why Ol' Hezekiah thought he was King of the World.

"He'll be back," Li'l said. "You just wait."

"I don't think I want to wait," I said. "What if he catches us here? He could think we're trying to steal his eggs. He could put a curse on us."

Both Li'l and Billy Royce turned and looked at me like I was somebody's little brother. They both shook their heads slowly and turned back to stare at the chicken coop. "Ain't no such thing as curses," Billy Royce said. "Don't be dumb."

"How do you know?" I asked. And that was a real question.

The longer we laid there in the grass looking at the chicken coop, the more I wanted Li'l or Billy Royce to convince me that there was no such thing as Ol' Hezekiah's curse. The more I looked at that sign, the more I wondered if Ol' Hezekiah might not have some kind of power. Then I thought of Otha Smith.

"What about Otha Smith?" I said.

"What about him?" Billy Royce answered.

"You were there on Main Street that night. Ol' Hezekiah told Mr. Otha that he was going to die and go to Hell because he was bad to drink. Maybe that was a curse."

"Old man Smith was seventy-five years old, and he had been drunk since before we were born. It don't take a curse to kill somebody like that."

I still wasn't convinced. Even though it was getting cooler because the sun was going down behind the railroad tracks, I was sweating. I could feel the sweat running down my neck into my gabardine shirt. I could also feel my heart pumping real hard. Like it was trying to tell me something. "I think I'm going to go," I told them.

Li'l glanced at me. "Chicken," he said. "You ought to be out there with them." He nodded in the general direction of the chickens pecking on the ground.

Billy Royce snorted. "Ah, let him go. If he's scared, he ought to go home. I'm going to stay and see if Ol' Hezekiah comes back. I still don't believe he lives here."

I was halfway up and halfway down, trying to decide whether it was better to stay here where I had company or walk back through the woods by myself. Suddenly, the decision was made for me.

"SINNERS!"

The voice boomed out from behind us, loud and rasping and absolutely convincing.

"SINNERS," it said again. Then, softer, but not a bit less frightening, "What are y'all doing about my eggs."

We turned around, and behind us, maybe fifteen feet away, was Ol' Hezekiah. From where we were, lying on the ground, he looked about fifteen feet tall. But we knew he wasn't real tall, no taller than my daddy. But that didn't help. Ol' Hezekiah had long gray hair that tangled down to his shoulders and a full gray beard that looked just like the one God wore in the picture in the Sunday School room. He wore two overcoats and brogan shoes. In one hand, he held a Bible, and in the other one, a show poster that he rolled up to yell through. And he stood just fifteen feet away.

"You trespass against me and against the Lord.

We were getting to our feet, slowly, without ever taking our eyes off Ol' Hezekiah. "We didn't do nothing," Billy Royce said.

"We didn't bother your old eggs," Li'l said.

I didn't say anything. We had been caught. We would be cursed. For a split second, I wondered if being cursed and going to Hell had to be the same thing. Maybe there was another kind of curse.

Then I felt Billy Royce grab my arm, and we were all running through the woods.

"SINNERS. YOU WILL PAY."

Ol' Hezekiah's voice followed us out of the woods and made us run a little faster. When we got to the weeds where we had hidden the skates, we flopped down on the ground, breathing hard. I could feel the pain in my side like something was trying to pull it apart. But Billy Royce was laughing, and Li'l had a big grin on his face.

"Told you," he said. "That's where Ol' Hezekiah lives."

Billy Royce nodded his head, still laughing. “Sinners,” he said, trying to sound like Ol’ Hezekiah. “I guess he’s right. We’re now officially sinners. Hezekiah said so.”

“Everybody’s a sinner,” I said. “It says so in the Bible. All men sin and come short of the glory of God. Paul said it.”

“Listen to the preacher man,” Li’l said. “Maybe you ought to get a show poster and stand outside the movie with Ol’ Hezekiah.”

“Don’t joke about things like that,” I said. “God hears everything.”

Billy Royce punched me on the shoulder. “You just worry too much. If God hears what we’re saying, I don’t think he cares very much. He sure don’t care if we go down and look at the King of the World’s chicken coop.” Then he started laughing again.

We got our skates out of the weeds and started walking home.

We didn’t hurry much because we knew we were all late for dinner, and we were probably all going to get some kind of punishment when we got home. Li’l’s daddy was the only one that still spanked him. We were twelve years old, and we thought we were too big to be spanked. Li’l’s daddy didn’t agree, and Billy Royce’s parents and my parents had come up with some pretty good substitutes. But if we were already too late, there wasn’t any use to hurry.

It was about six-thirty when I got home. Mama and Daddy were still at the kitchen table.

“Where you been, Jody?” Mother asked, not even turning her head to make sure it was me. “You just about missed supper.”

“We were skating. Went further than we thought. Took longer to get back.”

Daddy sort of grinned. “I guess you’re lucky. We’re having leftovers. That ought to be punishment enough.”

I just kept walking. Daddy teasing Mama about the leftovers wasn't anything new. Daddy didn't really like to eat leftovers, but about twice a week, Mama said she had to clean out the refrigerator, and we would have supper with three kinds of meat and maybe four kinds of vegetables. Whatever was left over from the last several days.

After putting my skates in my room and washing my hands, I went back to the kitchen and sat down. There was fried chicken, mashed potatoes, and a few butter beans from Sunday dinner. A thin, fried pork chop from Monday along with some green beans and squash and onions, and a couple of pieces of streak o'lean that I couldn't place. I took the pork chop, some butter beans, and squash. I got up and poured myself a glass of milk.

"You get into any interesting trouble today, bud?" Daddy was always trying to be funny. Sometimes he was.

"No trouble. Just Li'l, Billy Royce, and me. We went skating down toward the power plant."

"I guess there was a time when I thought skating two or three miles could be called fun. I don't remember when it was, though."

"How much homework do you have tonight, Jody?" Mother asked.

You could trust her to bring the conversation back to being responsible, doing my homework, or cleaning up my room. Especially since we had just gotten a television set. The rule was that I had to take care of all my responsibilities before I watched television.

"Not much. Some arithmetic. Spelling test is tomorrow."

"Well, when you finish supper, go study your spelling. Maybe your daddy can call out the words to you."

Daddy had finished his dinner and was wiping his mouth. He shook his head. "Not tonight. I have to go back down to the paper tonight and write something for the editorial page."

"Okay. I'll do it after I finish in the kitchen."

She and Daddy got up and took their plates to the sink, leaving me eating. Daddy gave Mama a hug and a peck on the cheek. "I should be back by ten."

Mama gave him a hug back. "I hope so. You're just too grumpy when you don't get enough sleep." They both sort of laughed, and daddy went out the back door. Mama started washing the dishes.

"Mama, is there any such thing as a curse?"

She stopped washing the dishes and turned around, wiping her hands on her apron. She looked like she was trying to figure out if I had really said what she thought I had said.

"What do you mean, Jody? What kind of curse?"

"I mean, could somebody put a curse on you and hurt you." She walked back over to the table and sat down, watching me very carefully. "I don't think so, Jody. Some people, like those people who practice voodoo, may believe that they can. But we don't believe that. We're Christians."

"Do we believe in Hell?"

She thought a minute. "Yes. We believe in Heaven, and we believe in Hell. You know what it says in the Bible. Why are you so interested in curses and Hell? You get involved in something you shouldn't have?"

I thought about telling her about our run-in with Ol' Hezekiah, but I didn't think about it for long. It could get real complicated when I tried to explain to Mama that I hadn't really done anything, but I was worried about what I had done. I just shook my head. "Li'l, and Billy Royce and I were talking about it. I don't think they believe in Hell."

Mama got up and went back to the sink. "At twelve years old, I don't think there's a whole lot of point in any of you worrying about it. There'll be time for that."

I went into my room and pulled out my arithmetic book and my spelling book, but before I started studying, I picked up my

Bible. It always stayed on my bedside table because I was supposed to read my devotional every night. Sometimes I did.

I looked in the back, in the Concordance. In Matthew 5:22, it said that if I called somebody a fool, I was in danger of hellfire. In Matthew 10:28, it said that I should fear him which is able to destroy both body and soul in Hell. Then in the next chapter, Jesus said Capernaum would be brought down to hell. In Matthew 23:15, Jesus was talking about the Pharisees making something called a proselyte into a "child of Hell." I kept looking up the places in the Bible that talked about Hell. There was the rich man pleading for water. There was the eternal fire.

The Bible had a lot to say about Hell, and that was just in the New Testament.

I was sitting there wondering about a fire that burned forever when Mama knocked on the door. "You ready for me to call out your spelling, Jody?"

"Just a minute, Mama. I'm almost finished."

"Okay, just bring it out when you're ready."

I put the Bible away and pulled out my spelling book. It was hard to concentrate on the spelling. "Character" doesn't seem important, at least spelling it doesn't, when you've been thinking about burning for eternity.

I got through my spelling and my arithmetic and was getting ready for bed when Daddy got back from the paper. He came in to tell me goodnight.

"Your mama tells me that you were asking her some questions about curses and hell. Anything we should be talking about, bud?"

"No, I just don't understand it. I can't understand just burning forever."

He patted me on the shoulder. "I don't think any of us can understand that. I don't."

"Don't you believe in Hell, Daddy?"

"I guess I do. It's in the Bible. So's Heaven. I'd rather think about Heaven."

"Preacher Cavanaugh said that if we didn't believe in Jesus and didn't do right, we would go to Hell." Preacher Cavanaugh was the preacher at our church. We're Baptist, what some people call "hard shell," whatever that means.

Daddy stopped and thought for a minute. He looked very serious, which was unusual for him.

"Jody, I don't know if this is the time for us to be talking about this. Maybe we should wait until you're older. But you asked, and I'm going to give you the best answer I can.

"I think some people, preachers mostly, try to scare people into being good, doing the right thing. They think that, if they convince us that something really bad, something so bad that we can't even imagine it, is going to happen to us if we don't do what they think is right, we'll do it. Just because we're afraid.

"If I understand it right, for everything in the Bible that talks about hell, there's something else, or maybe two or three things that talk about how much God loves us, and how he made us like him. I'd rather think we do the right thing and believe the right thing because God made some of him into us. Does that make any sense?"

"I guess so. I still don't understand it. How can God love us and throw us into a fire that burns forever." In one of my Sunday School lessons, the quarterly had said that if a bird went to a beach and picked up one grain of sand and carried it miles away, then came back and picked up another one, by the time he had moved the entire beach, the first minute of eternity would not have passed. How could something like burning go on and on?

"There'll be a lot of things in this world that you don't understand, Jody. After a while, you'll understand that you don't understand them, and you won't worry about them. Now, it's about time you read your devotional and went to sleep."

He kissed me on top of my head and left the room. I got my Bible, but instead of reading in Samuel about David, which was what my devotional was about, I read about Hell in Revelation. Then I turned off the light and thought about Hell. Would I go to Hell because I made Ol' Hezekiah mad? Or even if I stole some of his eggs? Did you go to Hell because you went to the pictures on Sunday? Or because you thought bad thoughts? By the time I finally went to sleep, I had about decided that if all the things I had been told were bad would make me go to Hell, I was surely going to Hell. The last thought I remember that night was Ol' Hezekiah standing over us in the woods with his big gray beard and his long gray hair, yelling, "SINNERS!"

The next morning my mind hadn't changed much, but I knew that before I went to Hell, I had to go to school. So I did everything I usually did—got dressed, ate my cereal, brushed my teeth, and walked to school—but while I did it, there was something deep down inside me that was different today than it was yesterday. Something that said I might be scared. On the way to school I said a prayer. "God, help me to know what I have to do not to go to Hell. Please."

That afternoon I told Li'l and Billy Royce that I couldn't go skating with them, that I had some chores to do. What I really wanted to do was talk to Ol' Hezekiah. I thought maybe if I told him I wasn't going to bother his eggs, he wouldn't be mad at me and wouldn't put a curse on me. But I knew if I told Li'l and Billy Royce, they would laugh at me.

Before I knew it, I was in the woods, staring at the chicken coop. "Cursed be anybody who steals my eggs." But I didn't steal his eggs. I didn't get close to his old eggs. What was I so worried about.

"What do you want, boy?"

The voice came from behind me, just like last time. But this time he wasn't yelling. He was just talking.

I turned around, and there he was, almost close enough to reach out and touch me. But he didn't. He just stood there in his two overcoats and brogan shoes.

"I don't want anything. I was just going to tell you that I wasn't going to steal your eggs yesterday. Really, I wasn't."

"What was you boys doing here, then?"

"We just came to see where you lived. Billy Royce, and Li'l and me."

"Well, you've seen it. Now, get on."

"I don't want you to be mad at us. You called us sinners, Mr. Hezekiah."

For the first time, it looked like his lips sort of turned up in a smile under the beard. Maybe nothing really moved, but his face looked different.

"You don't think you're a sinner, boy?"

"I know I am. It says in the Bible that everybody's a sinner."

"Read your Bible, do you?"

"Yes, sir. Every night."

"That's good."

We stood there a minute, looking at each other. I guess I looked as funny to him as he did to me. My ankles sticking out of my pants where I had grown so much, and my feet that had suddenly gotten too big for the rest of my body. At least if Ol' Hezekiah had shaved and taken off just one of those overcoats, he'd looked pretty normal. I worried about the fact that parts of me were growing at different times. Ol' Hezekiah started walking toward the chicken coop. After a couple of steps, he turned around.

"I'm tired now, boy. But you come back and talk to me sometime. We'll talk about the Bible."

When I got home, Mama was in the kitchen, rolling out dough for chicken stew. She smiled at me when I came in. "Your buddies were just here looking for you," she said.

"I've been downtown." I went to the refrigerator and got the milk. Mama handed me a glass. "Just don't spoil your supper. It's late."

"Okay," I said. I grabbed a hand full of vanilla wafers out of the box and went into the living room. I didn't think anything could spoil my breakfast, dinner, or supper. It seemed like I was always hungry lately, and since we had to eat at the new cafeteria at school where they served lunch, I didn't ever feel like I had had enough to eat until after supper at home.

The next day after school, we went to the movies at the Princess. The movie was Cisco Kid with a Three Stooges comedy and, of course, Nyoka, Queen of the Jungle. She got herself untied before the rope burned through and managed to use the rope to swing to safety just as it popped. Then she chased the bad hunters some more before she got in a fight with one on a raft in the river. He had knocked her down just as the raft went over a waterfall about two hundred feet high. We'd have to come back next week to see how she got out of that one.

When we left the movie, Ol' Hezekiah was standing right outside the door, yelling through his rolled-up show poster.

"MOVIN' PICTURES are the images of the DEVIL. MOVIN' PICTURES are a SIN and an ABOMINATION."

Everybody, mostly kids like us, just walked by him and didn't pay any attention. We were used to Ol' Hezekiah standing outside the picture show. But I looked at him, and when I did, he stopped yelling for a minute, and it looked to me like he smiled. Or maybe he didn't. But his face looked different.

It was already almost dark, so I went straight home. As I walked, I thought about Ol' Hezekiah. I wondered where he came from and why he didn't have a job like Daddy. Was he really crazy? When he just talked, instead of yelling, he didn't seem crazy.

Thursday and Friday were busy with school and Scouts and raking the leaves. But Saturday morning, when I got up, I knew

I was going to see Ol' Hezekiah. I had been thinking about him off and on all week. I didn't really think he had put a curse on me, but I still hadn't decided whether I thought I was going to Hell. Every now and then I would worry about it.

Daddy had already gone down to the paper when I got up, and Mama was getting ready for the ladies to come over and play Canasta at what they were calling lunch. She was just as happy for me to get out of the house.

I cut through the back yard and went down Hill Street to the highway and through the cemetery to the woods. I was coming up on Ol' Hezekiah's house or chicken coop from the back. But I made plenty of noise so that he wouldn't think I was trying to sneak up on him.

As I was pushing through the weeds and branches, I thought about the Nyoka in the jungle when she caught the bad hunters and could have thrown them down to the lions to eat. "I'm giving you a chance that you wouldn't give anybody else," she had said, as she tied them up. It sounded good. But later, they got away. Maybe she should have gone ahead and thrown them to the lions. Maybe giving them a chance wasn't a good idea.

When I got to Ol' Hezekiah's, he was in front of the chicken coop at a little fire. There was an old blackened coffee pot on the rocks at the edge of the fire. He was reading his Bible.

He looked up when he heard me. "So you came back," he said. "I wondered if you were going to."

"Yes, sir. You said I could come back to talk."

"Yeah. Well, have a seat. I guess you're too young to drink coffee."

I had been drinking coffee since I was six years old, but I decided that maybe it would be better if I didn't drink his.

"Thank you anyway," I said, sitting down on a log.

"You're a polite youngun. That's good. You're J.D. Powell's boy, aren't you?"

"Yes, sir." I was surprised that he knew me or even knew Daddy, although about everybody in Cranville knew Daddy. He was the editor of the paper. We sat quietly for a minute while he poured his coffee in a tin cup. He sipped it.

"You a Christian, boy? I know you told me you read the Bible, but that don't make you a Christian. You believe in Jesus Christ."

"Yes, sir, Mr. Hezekiah. I joined the church last year."

"It's good to join the church, but that don't make you a Christian either." He sipped his coffee again. Then I could have sworn that he laughed or chuckled or something. It was just a sound, but it was a sound like something inside him had struck him funny.

"I guess I can tell you. It's been a long time since I told anybody. Name's not Hezekiah. It's Amos. Amos Thomas."

"But, why do they call you Mr. Hezekiah?"

"They don't. Nobody calls me mister, except maybe you and that to my face. Mostly they call me Ol' Hezekiah. I'm old.

"I guess, because of the way I act and the way I look, they thought I ought to be called something out of the Old Testament. Showed some of them didn't read their Bible much. My real name, Amos, is a good Old Testament name. Amos was a prophet. Hezekiah was a king, but they probably thought he was a prophet. But since they called me a king name, I kept it."

He motioned to the words over the chicken coop door. "That's how come I painted that." He made that sound again, like a chuckle or a laugh.

"I thought it was just right. A king in a chicken coop. Like Jesus, who came into Jerusalem riding on a donkey. Yeah, it was just right."

The way he said it, he sounded like the whole thing was funny to him. "You don't think you're the King of the World?"

His head turned real quick, and he started to say something.

Then he stopped and took another sip of his coffee.

"No, I don't think I'm King of the World. There's not but one king. That's God and his son, Jesus. I was a farmer over in Sampson County. But I guess I spent more time reading my Bible than tending my crops, so I wasn't a good farmer. The people in my church didn't like me much either. I thought different from them. My wife left me. I lost my farm to Mr. Price over there who used to lend me planting money. So I didn't have any reason to stay there.

"When I got here, I felt like God had a reason for me to stay here."

"What's that, Mr. Hezekiah?"

He studied his coffee. "Call me Amos, son. Or Mr. Thomas if you want to. I'd like for somebody to call me by my right name, now. I don't know why I'm here. I believe that everybody is put someplace for a reason. God told me to come here. He told me to stay here. He hasn't told me why."

"Can you really put a curse on somebody?"

He looked at the painting over the door again. "No, but it keeps some people from stealing my eggs. That's mostly what I eat, and I trade some of them for coffee and bacon. I can't put a curse on anybody. People mostly put curses on themselves by what they do and not listening to what God wants them to do."

He poured himself some more coffee. "What do you like most in the Bible, boy?" He blew on the cup to cool it and waited for me to answer.

I started to say I liked all of it since the Bible was the word of God, and it might not sound good to say that there was one part I liked better than the other. But what I said was, "I like the stories in the Old Testament, the battles. And I like stories like David and Goliath and where Samson pulled down the building on the Philistines."

"You like it when the good wins out then."

"Yes, just like in the pictures." As soon as I said the word pictures, I wanted to cram it back in my mouth. I knew what he thought about picture shows. But he didn't say anything about it. He just kept looking at his coffee.

"Well, remember, boy. This is God's world, and good always wins out, even if it don't look like it sometimes. This is God's world."

He stood up slowly, like it hurt him to move. He threw the coffee in the bushes like the cowboys always did at the chuck wagon. "I got things I got to do. But I'm glad you come, boy. You keep reading your Bible. You keep being a Christian." He turned around and walked slowly back to the chicken coop. I knew it was time for me to go.

I walked back home, looking at the red and yellow leaves on the maple trees and the brown leaves on the oak trees. It was November, and all the leaves weren't gone yet. Mr. Thomas had said he thought everybody was put somewhere for a reason. I wondered what kind of reason God might have for me, and if I could figure it out or if God would tell me before it was too late. And I wondered what did make a Christian. I thought reading the Bible and going to church had something to do with it. I knew you had to believe in Jesus, but I figured you had to do something, too.

I went back to see Mr. Thomas a couple of times after school, but he wasn't there. And I saw him on the sidewalk outside the Princess, but we didn't talk. He would speak to me. He knew my name was Jody. And I would speak to him. It became so usual that Li'l and Billy Royce didn't even tease me about it.

When Thanksgiving came, I asked Mama if we had enough turkey and dressing for me to take some to Mr. Thomas. I had told Mama and Daddy about my going to see Mr. Thomas and how his name wasn't Hezekiah, but Mr. Thomas. They hadn't said much. They mostly listened.

"Do you think he would rather come have Thanksgiving dinner with us?" she asked.

I hadn't even thought of that. Somehow, the sight of Mr. Thomas with his long hair and long beard at our dinner table hadn't occurred to me.

"I don't know. Can I go ask him?"

"Go ask him. Tell him he'll be welcome, and we have plenty."

That Saturday morning, I went down to Mr. Amos's chicken coop. I went early, like I had before, and he was sitting out by his fire drinking his coffee.

We talked for a minute. He asked me if I had been reading my Bible, and I told him I had. Then I asked him if he wanted to come have Thanksgiving Dinner with Mamma, Daddy, and me on Thursday.

He did something I hadn't seen him do before. His face changed again, but he wasn't smiling or laughing. It looked like he almost cried. He looked down into his coffee cup.

"I don't think so, boy. It's been a long time since I sat down to eat with people, and I might not be able to do it right. But you tell your mama and daddy that I appreciate it. I really do."

"Well, could I bring you some turkey and dressing? We always have sweet potatoes and cranberry sauce. I could bring you a plate Thursday."

"That would be right nice. I don't know when I've had good turkey and dressing. My mother made it. My wife, she won't much of a cook. I guess I'd really like that."

We agreed that I would bring him his plate right after dinner on Thursday. He said he would be there.

The week went real quick, especially since we didn't have school on Wednesday, and the scouts took a hike down to Johnson's Cross Roads and back. That was almost twenty miles, and when we got back, our legs were aching, and all we wanted to do was go home.

But, on Thursday, we had Thanksgiving dinner just like we usually did. My uncle Fred and his wife came over. They hadn't been married long and didn't have any children. And Mama's sister, Beth Anne, who hadn't ever married, came. We all gathered around the dinner table in the kitchen.

After dinner, Mama got a paper plate out of the cabinet and piled turkey and dressing on it. She got another plate and put two sweet potatoes and some butter beans and some cranberry sauce on it. Then she put some tinfoil over both plates.

"Can you carry both of these, or do you think your daddy ought to give you a ride?"

I picked them up, and some of the butter bean juice ran down on my hand. She wiped it off and walked to the kitchen door.

"J.D., can you give Jody a ride to take this food to Mr. Thomas?"

Daddy had already sat down in the big chair and unbuckled his belt. He looked like he didn't want to get up, but he just nodded and buckled his belt back. "I'll be back in just a minute," he said to Uncle Fred.

He helped me carry the plates to the car, then we drove down Church Street to the road to the power plant. I started to tell him where to stop, but Daddy already knew. We got out, with him taking one plate and me taking the other one, and we walked through the woods to Mr. Thomas's house. The door was open, and the chickens were pecking at the dirt around it.

"Mr. Thomas," I called. I didn't see or hear him.

"He said he would be here," I said to Daddy. Daddy just nodded.

"Let me look in the house, Jody," he said. And he walked up to the door and peered in.

He put the plate down on the ground and went in the chicken coop. I walked up to the door.

It wasn't big. On one side, there were some boxes with some cups and plates and a few cans of food. Across the back, there was an iron cot. On the other side, there were the roosts for the chickens. There weren't any lights. All the light came in the door or in the space between the roof and the walls. When my eyes adjusted to the light, I saw Mr. Thomas was on the cot. Daddy was kneeling by him. He turned to me and shook his head.

I started to come in, but Daddy held out his hand. "I don't think you should come in, Jody." Then he stopped. "Maybe you should. He was your friend."

I walked up to the cot, and Mr. Thomas lay there with his eyes closed. He looked like he was sleeping. "He's dead, isn't he?"

Daddy nodded. "He was an old man. He told me he was tired."

I was surprised. "You talked to him." Somehow, I thought that I was the only one who ever talked to him.

"Sometimes. Sometimes when I was working late at the paper, he would come in and have a cup of coffee with me, and we'd talk."

"You never told me."

"There wasn't any reason to. He came by. We talked. I tried to give him some clothes one time, but he said he couldn't do that. I don't know that he ever took anything from anybody. Your friend had some dignity."

I looked at Mr. Thomas again. It was the first time I had ever seen anybody dead except in the moving pictures. But it didn't look bad. His face looked like it did when he looked at me, and it changed like he was smiling.

Daddy took one of the overcoats that were lying on him and pulled it up over his face. He saw that I was still holding the plate of turkey and dressing.

"Leave the food, Jody. We need to go get Mr. Williams to come get Mr. Thomas. We need to get him buried."

I put the plate down on the floor of the chicken coop, and Daddy and I walked back through the weeds to the car. I had to stop and look back.

"Daddy, Mr. Thomas told me he thought God told him to stop here for a reason. I wonder what that reason was."

"That's another thing we don't know, Jody. I imagine he was put here for a reason, but we don't know what it was."

But I couldn't help but wonder.

The Measure of Morton Findlay

Morton Findlay wore his ordinariness like a badge of honor. For nearly all of his life, he had determinedly stayed at the very center of any spectrum he encountered. He was neither tall nor short, light nor dark, slender nor heavy. When he was eight, his teacher had asked him what he wanted to be when he grew up. He told her he would like to be an insurance salesman or maybe a bottled water truck driver.

It wasn't that he was descended from particularly ordinary people. In fact, his brother was a doctor well respected by his colleagues and most of his patients. His sister was a television anchorperson in the 28th largest market in the United States. His mother had won a ribbon—either green or gold—at a county fair when she was only eighteen. But, in the midst of all that accomplishment, some recessive gene injected into the pool by a distant, very ordinary ancestor claimed Morton at a very early age and guided his every decision until the present day, when he was a clerk in men's furnishings in a department store. He was known for the number of brown suits and solid dark brown ties he sold.

It was not a bad life, a flat line of contentment interrupted infrequently by questioning calls from his mother or sly criticism from his brother or sister. They always wanted to know when he was going to *do* something. But Morton knew that he was doing something: avoiding the abrasive world where people who tried to be extraordinary were worn down to shadows, just as one day his brother and sister would be.

All of that was true until September 9, 2005 at approximately three o'clock. Morton was refolding and stacking pants according to waist size when she came in, walking quickly, a blur of blond hair, very red lipstick, a royal blue scarf that wrapped around her neck and fell nearly to her knees. She looked around quickly, her gaze shooting from one rack of suits to another. Her gaze passed Morton, went to another rack of suits, and repassed him on the way back, never indicating that she had seen him. Nor that she had seen him staring at her with his mouth agape and his eyes much wider than usual, as a man stricken.

She started to turn to leave, but he summoned the strength to take the three steps required to reach her side.

"May I help you with something?" he said, amazed that the words came out with some hint of intelligence. His mouth seemed to be operating independently of his mind.

She turned and looked at him.

"I'm looking for a suit. You don't seem to have what I'm looking for."

"We do have an extensive inventory. Perhaps, if you'll tell me just what you want, I can help you find it."

Morton realized that he was reciting the salesperson's catechism even as he inventoried her. The striking blue eyes. The very clear complexion. The straight nose. Everything exactly as it should be for the greatest beauty.

"I want a really ugly suit in size 41 long," she said. "Maybe something in a loud plaid or a wide chalk stripe."

"I beg your pardon. Did you say 'ugly suit.'"

"Yes. The uglier, the better. And I don't care how much it costs."

A sudden burst of loyalty for his employer almost caused Morton to declare that H.B. Tucker and Co. did not carry ugly suits, only beautifully crafted suits of the very best quality. But the idea of causing this image to disappear stopped him. Some part of him wanted to prolong this conversation for every possible minute.

He looked thoughtful.

"I see. There may be something in the back that will meet your needs." He pointed to a row of chairs in the shoe department. "Would you care to wait over there while I see what I can find?"

She nodded and walked away, her blue scarf swaying with each step. Tearing his eyes from her, he hurried to the back past the boxes waiting to be opened, past the partially dismembered mannequins to a seldom-visited space where forgotten inventory laid or hung, a history of what would not sell even when marked down for the second, third, or fourth time. Digging into ancient history, Morton found what he thought he had remembered: a suit from the '70s. A pale blue and green plaid with lapels that reached almost to the edge of the shoulder pads.

Convinced that there was no uglier suit in the store, he pulled it from the rack. It was, he thought, the worst of an era of extremely bad fashion. He brushed the dust from the collar and shoulders and carried the suit to the front.

"I believe that this might meet your needs," he said.

She stood up, slightly squinting her eyes as she looked at the suit. She reached out and touched the lapels.

"Yes. I believe it just might."

The thought had been worming around in his mind since she had made such a point about needing an ugly suit. The counter thought was that it was none of his business, and the counter to that was that the longer he could engage her in this transaction, the longer he could be in the presence of this beautiful woman. This was a desire that Morton had never experienced before, and he didn't know that he liked it now, but it was there, like it or not.

"May I ask, why you specifically want...as you say...an ugly suit? Is this for a costume party or something?"

"Something like that. I'm going as a grieving widow. He's going as a dead man. This is my husband's burial suit."

"Oh, your husband. I'm sorry."

She shook her head. "Don't be. He was a pig. Thought it was fun to drag me around the room by my hair. I'll take the suit."

"I'm sorry."

"You say that a lot, don't you."

"I ... I just..."

"Don't worry about it.

Morton pulled a suit bag from the roll beside the counter.

"How did he die?"

"Pretty much the same way he lived. We were sitting at the dinner table, and he was shoveling food in his mouth, feeding like a pig. Suddenly, he was not making any noise, just jumping up and down and pointing to his throat. I think he was turning a little blue."

"My goodness. What did you do?"

"I went to the drug store. Bought a bottle of nail polish and a new lipstick."

Morton couldn't think of anything else to say except, "that'll be a hundred and eighty dollars, plus tax."

She gave him her credit card, and Morton completed the transaction. It occurred to him that he could get her name from the credit card. Maybe he could call her after a decent time and ask to see her. Maybe he could experience this quickening of his heartbeat again. Then it occurred to him; he didn't really want to do that.

She took her receipt and left. Morton turned back to the pants he was stacking. There was, he thought, something to be said for avoiding the abrasive world of people who tried to do something.

One of God's Finest Creations

It weren't much different from where I lived.

It was just one room. Where I lived up in Flat Tree Gap was one room. And there was just one window. Just like my cabin. I suppose the difference was there was a lock on the door here. I didn't have one at the cabin. And here they wouldn't let me come and go like I wanted to.

In the morning, they let me out, and I mopped the floors in the hall in front of the cells, and I mopped all the empty cells. Mostly they were empty, except on weekends when they brought in two or three who were afflicted with moonshine. I knew most of them. I'd sold them corn liquor.

It was in the afternoon, and—best I could figure—I only had twelve days left. I'd been here for seventy-eight days, and the judge gave me ninety days. That was a few more than he usually did. I guess that he was just tired of seeing me. I'd made the scratches on the bunk, one for each day I was here so that I could keep up with it. One time before they'd made me change cells, so I lost count. This time there were seventy-eight scratches on the corner I was using.

I was just laying there, thinking about how I'd get the copper I needed for my new still. The sheriff's people had chopped up my old one. Maybe they had sold off the copper. Either way, I didn't have it, and I couldn't get it. I still hadn't figured it out when Kenton showed up at my door. Kenton was one of the sheriff's deputies, and he stayed around the jail most of the time.

Kenton was a big man, mostly in his belly and his legs. His legs were so fat that he had to walk with them spread apart. Sort of like a duck.

"Get up, Ethan," he said. "I got to take you somewhere."

I shook my head. "Nah. I already mopped the floors. That's all they said I had to do."

"Ain't got nothing to do with mopping. Get out of the bunk and come on."

I didn't like the sound of that. I didn't think the sheriff was going to put me on a road gang. I just had twelve days left. Besides, he didn't have enough prisoners to make a road gang. But I got up and walked to the door. About as slow as I could.

Kenton unlocked the door and walked down the hall. Didn't say another word. Didn't look back to see if I was coming with him. We walked by the empty cells, through the jail door, and into the sheriff's office.

Bailey Adams, the sheriff, was sitting back in his chair with his feet up on his desk. I always thought it was a mark of the sheriff's good character that he still wore brogans. He was not one for putting on airs. Bailey'd been sheriff about as long as I had been a bootlegger, and generally, we got along. Every few years, sometime before the elections came, he'd have to arrest somebody. Sometimes it would be me. It was sort of a show. He'd make a big deal out of chopping up a still, and he'd usually get his picture taken pouring out the shine.

I knew that, even when he had me in handcuffs somewhere behind him in the picture, it wasn't my moonshine he was pouring out. He kept that for himself and his family. There were enough bad moonshiners around that he didn't have to pour out the good stuff.

"How ya doin', Ethan?" he said.

"Tolerable," I said.

"You rehabilitated yet?"

"Don't know. Have to wait and see, I guess."

"I guess," he said. He took his feet off his desk and leaned toward me.

“Got something I need for you to do,” he said. “Might not be something you want to do. Don’t know. If you don’t want to, you don’t have to.”

It wasn’t like Bailey to beat around the bush like that. I wasn’t sure I liked it. Nice thing about being in jail was I didn’t have to make a lot of decisions. But I couldn’t help being a little curious about what Bailey was beating around the bush about. So I just stood there.

“I got Joe Spivey in the solitary cell. He’s going to be hung this afternoon.” From the look on Bailey’s face, I could tell he didn’t like the idea.

“Hung? What’d he do?”

“I let Joe tell you that. I told him I’d get him a preacher, but he said that he didn’t want one. I told him you were here. He said you’d be alright.”

Joe and I had been neighbors, but up in the Gap, that meant he’d lived two or three miles from me. We’d talked sometime and seen each other in town. But Joe and I, we didn’t spend a lot of time together. He didn’t drink. He went to church. He was married, and best I could tell, he was glad of it. Not much in common between us. But if Joe wanted me instead of his preacher or some other preacher, it was about the least I could do for a man about to get hung.

I nodded, and Bailey nodded.

“Come on, then,” Kenton said. He left the office. I followed along.

I’d never been in this part of the jail. Nobody gets hung for moonshining. Sixty days. Maybe ninety days. That’s all there is. That’s the reason I never truly thought about giving up making liquor. It’s what I knew how to do. What my daddy did. And it made me enough to live on. Didn’t need much since nobody wanted to marry me, and I didn’t want to get married.

There were only two cells, and one of them was empty. They were both kind of dark. Kenton unlocked the one on the right, and I heard somebody stirring.

"Hey, Ethan." I still couldn't make out who it was, but I figured it must be Joe.

"Hey, Joe. Hear you got yourself in a mess."

"I guess. Won't be much of a problem much longer. They going to hang me at three."

I didn't know what time it was, but I knew I'd eaten. That meant it was probably getting close to three.

Now I could see Joe. He was sitting on the edge of his bunk and had his elbows on his knees. He was just staring at the wall. Joe was always a skinny sort, but now all I could see was his knobby wrists sticking out of the sleeves that were hanging off his bony shoulders. Like somebody had sucked all the flesh right off of him. I wondered how a man that skinny could make an honest living. He shifted down a little so I could sit down on his bunk.

I sat down and stared at the wall with him for a minute. It seemed like what he wanted to do. But I couldn't help wondering what he'd done that was bad enough for them to hang him.

"How did you get into this mess, Joe?"

"Wasn't hard. I killed Avery Spence. Then I walked into town and told the sheriff what I'd done."

"Damn! When was this?"

"Little over a week ago. On a Tuesday, I think."

"And they're going to hang you today? That's real quick."

"Don't take long. 'Bout the only thing I said to the judge was I did it. Seemed to be enough."

"Well, maybe if you had a good reason, they wouldn't hang you for it."

"I guess my reason was good enough. I guess hanging's good enough, too. I don't want to go down to Alto for the rest of my life."

He went back to staring at the wall. I did too. But in a minute, there was something else I wanted to know.

"Why did you kill Avery Spence?"

"Seemed like the thing to do."

I thought maybe he had some kind of better reason than that, but before I could ask him what, he started talking again.

"You know Nancy?"

I did. Nancy Spivey had one time been the best looking woman in the Gap. She still was prettier than most. She had long hair that bounced on her back when she walked. A little waist. Hips that went back and forth at the ends of her hair. Most everybody, especially the men, knew Nancy Spivey. Some of them probably thought of her some. I didn't. Not just because she was married to Joe Spivey, but because I couldn't figure out why Nancy Spivey would want anything to do with me.

She had some education. She'd been to the school up at the Gap until she finished there. That was eight years. Then she helped her mama on the farm after her daddy died. Then she married Joe Spivey, and he took over running the farm.

"Yeah, I know Nancy, but what's that to do with Avery Spence."

"She took up with him. Behind my back. Maybe he took up with her. Anyway, they were together."

"You mean she was running around with Avery Spence?"

"I think I said that."

"And you shot him for it?"

"Nope. That won't the reason. I figure she was about as much responsible as he was for the running around. If I was going to shoot one of them, I'd had to shoot them both."

I could see how he was right about that. One did about the same thing as the other, in a general way. Seemed like reason enough. I heard him make a noise. When I looked, his bony shoulders were shaking, and he had his face stuck in his hands. I moved a little further away on the bunk. In a minute, he wiped his face on his sleeve.

"I loved her. I couldn't of killed her, no matter what she did."

He wiped his face again, dragging his sleeve across his eyes.

"You know, I never could figure out why she married me. I know I'm not a lot to look at. I never had a lot of money. There was something. Her mama said it was because I knew how to plow a rocky field and get corn in the ground. Maybe that was all there was to it. If it was, I didn't care. I figured whatever made her want me in her bed, whatever made her want me at her table, that was good enough. I didn't ask no questions.

"But she changed. I thought it was something I'd done. But it didn't matter what I said or what I did; she still didn't seem like she used to. I'd try to be warm. She'd just turn away. Then she started going out. Never said where she was going. I'd just sit home and wait for her to come back.

"One night when she left, I went after her. Just to see where she was going. She walked down the path and around the edge of the creek. Then she crossed it and went into the woods."

We heard a noise at the door and saw Kenton standing there.

"Here's that peach you wanted, Joe. You sure you don't want something else."

Joe shook his head and got up to walk over to the door. He took the peach from Kenton through the bars. He looked at it, then rubbed it on his shirt sleeves.

"No, thank you, Kenton. I don't reckon I'll be around long enough to get real hungry. Obliged to you."

"You let me know if you decide you want something else, Joe. Everybody should get a last meal."

Joe held up the peach.

"This'll do fine."

He sat back down on the bunk, looking at the peach.

"You know," he said, "there's nothing much better than a ripe peach. I'm gonna miss that. Sweet with peach juice running down my chin. One of God's finest creations."

He took a little bite of the peach and wiped his mouth on his sleeve.

"You followed Nancy into the woods?"

"Yep. Not hard to follow somebody who don't know they're being followed. I just walked real quiet and stayed a ways behind her. Nancy came into a clearing and just stopped and sat down on the ground. I thought maybe she just came out here to think. I do that sometimes. But then Avery Spence comes up. Nancy gets up and kisses him. She kissed him harder than she'd kissed me in a long time, maybe ever. Then they lay down on the ground, and Avery started putting his hands on her."

"What'd you do, Joe."

"Nothing. I just stayed behind the tree and watched. I watched, and when they finished and stood up, I crawled away."

I didn't know how a man could watch another man take his wife. I'd never had a wife. Never really had a girlfriend. I don't know what I would have done, but it wouldn't of been just to watch.

"If you didn't kill him for that, why'd you kill him?" I asked.

He just sat there, taking little bites out of the peach, wiping the juice off his chin.

"I followed her there two more times. I wanted to say something, do something, but I didn't know what. I just knew that I didn't want to lose my Nancy. Then the third time I followed her down there, hunkered down behind that tree, something was different. When he came into that clearing, she didn't kiss him. She just stood there.

"I watched Avery Spence come over to her and grab her by the shoulders. She shook her shoulders, trying to get his hands off her. Then she said something. I don't know what it was, but I could tell she was mad. He still had hold of her shoulders. She said something else, and he shook her. I thought he was going to break her neck.

"Then he hit her. Avery Spence hit my Nancy, and she went down on the ground. He just turned around and walked away. I wanted to run to her, but I couldn't let her know that I followed her. I stayed there 'til she got up and wiped off her face. Then I went back. Made like I was asleep. After a while, she came in and got in bed. I think she was still crying.

"I laid there, thinking about Avery Spence, and in my mind, I saw him hit Nancy again and again. She kept falling on the ground crying. The more I thought, the madder I got. I guess I figured out what I needed to do. When Nancy finally went to sleep, I got up, took two shotgun shells out of the box, and went to the barn.

"It ain't hard to make a slug for a shotgun. You just empty the shot out of the shell. Then you pour in some melted lead. In a while, you got a lead slug that'd kill most anything if you can hit it. It'd take down a bear. I made two slugs, then I got my shotgun and cut across the field and through the woods to Avery Spence's house. It was just about getting light.

"I put the two slugs in my double barrel and settled me down behind a bush between his back door and the outhouse.

"It wasn't long, right after first light, when he came out the back door, still in his nightshirt, scratching and yawning. He was walking toward the outhouse when I stood up and yelled out his name.

"He turned around, looked at me, and said 'What?'

"That's when I shot him. Shot him in the face, and that slug near took his head off his shoulders. Then I walked up to him and shot him in the dick with the second slug. There wasn't a whole lot left. Then I walked to town and told the sheriff what I'd done."

I just sat there for a minute, trying to get a picture of headless, dickless Avery Spence in my head. Couldn't feel sorry for him though, messing with Joe's wife like that. I knew that Joe could forgive her for going to Avery Spence, but he couldn't forgive Avery for hitting her. I didn't know whether that was real love or real crazy. Didn't much matter now.

"Would you do me a favor, Ethan?" he asked

I told him I would, but it'd be twelve days before I got out. Could it wait that long?

He said it probably couldn't, but maybe I could tell the sheriff.

"I want a decent burial," he said. "Probably not in the churchyard. Don't think they'd have much use for a cold-blooded murderer, no matter what the cause. But in a nice place. There's a hill on the farm that would make a good resting place, not far from the house with a big oak for shade. If Nancy wanted to, she could come visit it. I'd like to think she would. And would you tell her that right up 'til I quit breathing, I loved her? Don't make no difference what happened."

"Yeah, I'll talk to the sheriff, and I'll talk to Nancy. Did she come see you?"

"No. I asked the sheriff to tell her not to. I didn't want her to see me locked up. I know I was never much, but I was never behind bars."

He took another bite of the peach.

We heard a noise in the hall, and Kenton was unlocking the door.

"Time to go, Joe," he said. Kenton's voice was just about a whisper.

"Can Ethan walk with me?"

“Yeah, you get somebody to go with you. Usually, it’s a preacher.”

“Rather have Ethan, I think. Can’t imagine a preacher would want much to do with me now.”

“You might be surprised, Joe,” I said. I thought about some of the other people I’d seen go to the little church and what I knew about them. I thought some of them were a lot worse than Joe Spivey. He’d done one real bad thing, and he had cause. Some of those other folks did bad things about every day, for no good reason except they wanted to. That was part of the reason I didn’t go to church.

We walked down the hall, Kenton in front, then Joe, then I followed along behind. At the end of the hall, there was a thick wood door, probably about twice as thick as most. Kenton pushed it open and walked in.

The hanging room wasn’t big, maybe 10 feet each way. In the middle, there was a rope, a noose, and some kind of cutout thing on the floor. The hangman, Tommy Gomer, was standing just the other side of it. The sheriff was standing next to the door. Joe walked in and looked around. He nodded to Tommy and the sheriff.

“Tommy. Sheriff.”

They both nodded back. The sheriff walked up beside Joe.

“Here’s how it works, Joe,” he said. “You know what the noose is for. That square on the floor is a trap door, about six feet of space under it. When Tommy puts the noose on, and you say any last words you want to say, he’ll pull that lever over on the wall. The trap door’ll open, and you’ll drop through the hole. The noose will break your neck, so it’ll be over quick.”

Joe nodded. “That’s good.”

Then he stepped onto the trap door and looked at Tommy.

“Might as well do it, Tommy.”

Tommy put the noose over his head and tightened it up.

"Do you have any last words you want to say, Joe?" Bailey asked.

"Some. I asked Ethan to tell you about my last wishes, and I'd take it as a favor if you could do that."

Bailey nodded.

"And I want to thank Ethan for coming and sitting with me. I told you and the judge what I did, but I never told anybody why. Telling somebody, that was important to me."

He turned and looked at me.

"Thank you, Ethan. You done a kindly thing."

Then he held out the half of a peach that was left.

"I'd like for you to take this. It'd be a shame for half a good peach to go to waste."

I took the peach out of his hand. He looked at Tommy and nodded. Tommy pulled the lever for the trap door. The sheriff was right. It was over quick, and Joe Spivey just hung there, as dead as Avery Spence. We watched while his body swayed back and forth at the end of the rope. He had sort of a surprised expression on his face.

Tommy told us that we could leave, that he'd wait for the doctor to pronounce Joe dead. That was just something that had to be done.

So we all walked back into the hall, Bailey, Kenton, and me, leaving Joe dead and Tommy waiting for the county to say so. We didn't talk on the way back to the other part of the jail except for Bailey to ask me what Joe's last wishes were. I told him about the place on the farm where he wanted to be buried. I told him that he hoped that Nancy would visit the grave, though I didn't much think she would. I thought she'd left Joe a long time ago.

Bailey said he'd take care of it and that I could go get my stuff. I told him that I still had twelve days, and he said that I'd miscounted. I'd done a good thing today, and that had to count for something.

I went back to my cell and sat on my bunk. Eating the last half of Joe Spivey's peach. He was right. A good peach is one of God's finest creations.

The Spirit of Ava Gardner

By the time his scarred brown brogan hit the edge of the two-track path that May morning, Cory Messer knew that he was just going to keep walking. That time of the morning, the grass growing up between the tracks, still dew-wet, whisked the legs of his overalls, and the air had just a little bit of the heat that would wrap itself around him in a few hours.

This was the same path he went up every day, getting to the tobacco field or the cotton or the vegetable garden beyond the cotton. Some days he had a hoe over his shoulder, and some days he was on the old Farmall F-30. It was nearly 20 years old, but it would still pull a disc-harrow. But today was different. He didn't have his tools. He wasn't going to the fields. He was just going.

Cory didn't know where he was walking to, but he knew what he was walking away from. There was Agnes, his wife, and the angry words she'd shouted at him last night. There was Junior, the son he'd hoped to raise to be a good farmer, but no matter what Cory did, he couldn't make Junior feel the pride of being on his own land. Cory was the first of his people in memory to farm his own land. His daddy and granddaddy had farmed on shares and lived as best they could from one crop to the next. He'd tried to convince Junior to take some pride in it, but Junior didn't seem to care.

Cory walked. Head down. Shoulders bowed forward. He had always stood up straight since he had become a man at about thirteen or fourteen. His mama and his daddy had spent a lot of time teaching him how to be a man. To keep his word. To help his neighbor. To show respect and demand respect. Going to church and reading the Bible. But somewhere in the last three or four years, when it seemed that bad years followed one after another, he felt like the world was wearing down on him, pushing his head down, bowing his shoulders, and mashing something inside him so hard that sometimes he thought would explode.

Cory Messer was a tall, stringy man. His arms, sticking out from his rolled-up sleeves, showed the muscles and tendons, and every time he swallowed, his Adam's apple bobbed up and down. He was a man with nearly no belly or butt but with long legs that held them a ways off the ground. Usually, when he walked, it looked like he was stepping over corn rows, but today he walked one plodding step after another, his eyes toward the ground.

Cory pulled a pack of Chesterfields out of his overall pocket, tapped out a cigarette, and lit it, not giving much thought to any of the actions, slowly turning the pages of his life. He thought he'd done alright when he married Agnes. She stood to get well over a hundred acres when her daddy died, and old man Turner had been sickly when they got married. He died just a little after that. But that was more than fifteen years ago. Now he was thirty-five years old, the acreage had shrunk to about seventy, and it seemed that neither his wife nor his son thought much of him.

He looked at the tobacco field off to the right of the path. The tobacco had already been transplanted, and the young plants stretched from the path to the trees nearly a quarter of a mile away. The farm still had a six-acre allotment, and in a good year, that was enough to give them cash to get through the winter and to plant in the spring. But it seemed like good years were becoming more and more scarce. When he looked at it, he didn't see money; he saw nematodes and root rot.

On the left side of the path, he had cotton. He wondered why he even bothered with that. There wasn't much of a market anymore, not like when he was a boy. And he was pretty sure that the cotton they had cost them more than they made.

He just glanced at the cotton field. There was no point in pondering it. Times were changing. Everywhere. He'd heard that a bunch of people in Washington had decided that race-mixing in school was right. That wasn't what Cory believed or what his daddy and mama believed. Cory couldn't think of a single thing that was changing for the good.

The cigarette had burned almost down to his fingers. He threw it in the path and stepped on it as he walked by. He didn't have any idea where he was walking to, but he damn well knew what he was walking away from. He was walking away from being Agnes Messer's hen-pecked husband and Junior Messer's daddy and somebody who wasn't welcomed into the stores in River Falls because he sometimes had trouble paying his bills and had quit going to church.

It was about four miles to River Falls, but he didn't want to go to River Falls. It was about seven miles to Jamesville, but a lot of people knew him there, too. So, when he came to the intersection, he went straight, towards Smithfield. He figured that nobody knew him there or really wanted to. That would be a good place to be.

After an hour or so, Cory began to wonder if just walking away had been much of a plan. He had about ten dollars in his pocket, a part of a pack of Chesterfields, no food, and no water. He also had the clothes on his back and the straw hat on his head. Then he thought about the farm, and Agnes and Junior, and just kept walking.

Cory wondered if Agnes had missed him yet. He doubted it. She was probably scrubbing down the oilcloth on the kitchen table for the third time that morning.

After a while, he saw a woman sweeping her front yard with a brush broom. He walked up, took off his hat, and asked her if he could have some water. She motioned him toward the well and went on sweeping. A couple of hours later, he stopped at a crossroads store and bought some cheese and crackers. Back outside, he sat in the shade of the store for a few minutes, eating the cheese and crackers and drinking cool water from the pump. Then he got back on his way.

It was still early enough in the day that the shadows of the tall trees reached out toward Cody like fingers. At first, he avoided them, but as the day got hotter, Cory decided he should walk in the shade. Sometimes, he stumbled over a root or stepped in a hole, but the protection of the shade more than made up for it. He looked up at the sun, figuring it was somewhere around ten o'clock.

Cory stumbled on one more root, caught himself, and decided it was time to sit down for a minute. He found the trunk of a fallen-down tree, leaned up against it. The sweat was streaming down his cheeks and neck. There was no telling how hot and damp it would get as the day wore on. He wiped his face with his handkerchief and leaned his head back against the log.

Then he heard something behind him. He couldn't tell if it was an animal or a person. Cory peered around the tree, and on the other side, just a few feet away, a woman was sitting on the ground, a brown suitcase, cardboard trying to look like leather, beside her. She was trying to sob silently, but about every third one would sneak out. That's what Cory had heard.

He couldn't tell whether she knew he was there or not. If she did, she didn't make any sign. His first thought was just to move along, leave the woman to her sobbing, but that went against the way he was raised.

From what he could tell, she was young. She had on a blue dress, probably a nice one, but it was dirty, and there was a small torn place on the left shoulder. Her long brown hair fell down her back. She looked like she had been a well-kept person but wasn't doing well now.

He slid across the tree stump and edged up to her.

"You okay?"

Her head jerked up, and for the first time, he could see her face. It was pretty. Young. She had a wide mouth, and her nose was small. Everything about her face had been neatly placed, but her eyes were red and puffy from crying. She pushed herself to her feet and stepped away from him, leaving the suitcase between them.

He stopped and held up his hand, palm out, like an Indian.

"I ain't going to hurt you," he said. I just asked if you were okay. You hurt or something."

She shook her head.

"No, I'm okay. Thank you." She looked over her shoulder and took another step back.

Cory backed up and sat down on the tree trunk. The girl seemed to relax, just a little bit.

"You don't look okay, sitting here in the woods crying."

She looked at him for a moment, then she smiled a very small smile. As small as it was, it was the biggest smile any woman had given Cory in a while.

"I guess I don't," she said. She looked down at her dress, and her hands made quick gestures to smooth the wrinkles from it.

"I'm lost. And I'm out of money. And, I guess I don't know where I'm going or how I'm going to get there."

Cory nodded. He turned it over in his mind for a minute.

"Well," he said, "that makes about two of us. Except for the lost part. I know where I am. Between River Falls and Smithfield. Not far enough from one or close enough to the other. All I know to do is just keep walking."

"That's good.," she said. "Least you know where you are."

They sat there, not talking.

"How'd you get here, way out in the woods?" he asked.

She edged a little closer and sat down by her suitcase.

"It's a right long story," she said.

"We got some time. I'm still cooling off."

She nodded.

"I got on a bus in Albany. Albany, Georgia. And I got to Atlanta. I thought I'd stay in Atlanta, but I met a man who said there wasn't any work in Atlanta, but he'd take me to Spartanburg, and he could probably help me get a job in one of the mills."

"You're a long way from Spartanburg," he said. He'd never been there, but he knew it was in South Carolina. "How'd you end up here."

She just shook her head. He saw tears start running down her cheeks. She wiped her tears with her hands, then hugged herself around the waist. She looked at the ground, shaking her head from side to side.

"He never was going to take me to Spartanburg. He just told me that so I'd get in the car with him. He talked about how he'd get us a nice motel room and a fine meal. Then we'd have us some fun. It took me a few minutes to figure out what he was talking about. Where I come from, men don't say things like that to nice girls. Maybe he didn't think I was a nice girl. I don't know where he was taking me, but when he stopped for gas at that station up the road, I got out and ran."

Corey stared at the ground, trying to get a picture of a man who'd take a white woman like that. He just shook his head.

"Did he chase you?"

"No. I was down in the woods before he came out of the gas station. I ran down as deep as I could. Fell down some." She touched the torn place on the shoulder of her dress. "That's how I tore my dress. Tore up my stockings, too. I just threw them away."

For the first time, Cory noticed that her legs were bare. He felt something sort of stir, but not much.

"So what are you going to do now?" he asked.

"I don't know. That's why I was sitting here. I don't have any kind of plan." She looked out at the highway. "Where did you say we were."

"There's a town called River Falls about four miles back that way. Little bitty place. I don't think you'd find work there. Then there's Jamesville, over yonder, probably about six miles. Not much there either. And straight ahead, there's Smithfield. Fair sized place. Might be work there."

"But how would I get there?"

Cory thought that was just like a woman, asking a question that she already knew the answer to. He shrugged.

"I'm walking there. I might be able to hitch a ride. Probably be easier for me to hitch something if you're with me. But we may have to walk a long ways first."

She stuck out her leg, showing him her shoes. The heels weren't real high but probably too high to walk to Smithfield in.

"Don't know what to do about that," he said, "unless you can walk barefooted."

"I guess I'll have to see. No way I'm going to walk far in these."

She pulled off her shoes, opened her bag, and shoved them inside. Cory noticed that she had pretty ankles, and her toenails were painted red.

"I expect we better get going," he said. "Might be able to hitch a ride." He started walking off toward the road, and he heard her behind him. He stopped and took her suitcase out of hand. She seemed a little hesitant to let go of it, but she did.

As soon as they walked from under the trees, they felt the sun beat down on them, and it didn't take but a few minutes before Cory felt the sweat running down between his shoulder blades. He looked a the woman. She was staring straight ahead as she walked and hadn't broken a sweat.

"I don't know your name," he said.

"It's Annie. Annie Langdon."

"Pleased to meet you, Annie. I'm Cory. Cory Messer."

They walked some more, occasionally getting a cooling breeze from a passing car or truck speeding by. When a car came heading toward Smithfield, Cory stuck out his thumb and tried to look trustworthy. Nobody even slowed down.

They'd been walking for about an hour when Cory looked over his shoulder and saw a truck coming, heading for Smithfield. He held out his thumb, and the truck pulled off the blacktop and rolled to a stop. Cory could see that the back of the truck was loaded with vegetable crates. He and Annie rushed up to the truck, and Cory opened the door. The driver was a man about Cory's age, a cigarette hanging from his mouth.

"Hold on," the man said. Ain't got room for but one of you. I'll give the woman a ride, but I don't have room for you."

Cory saw that there was a box stacked on the seat. There wasn't much room, so he nodded to Annie to get in. Annie took a step back.

"Thank you anyway. But I don't want to leave my friend here." She closed the truck door.

"Suit yourself," the driver said and pulled off.

Cory watched as the trucked lumbered back on the blacktop, then sped down the road.

"What'd you do that for? He could have taken you to Smithfield."

She smiled the biggest smile he'd seen on her.

"Maybe I've already gotten in one car with a man I didn't know. That didn't work out. Or maybe I figured it wasn't nice to run off and leave somebody who had been nice to me. We'll get a ride. Or we'll walk to Smithfield."

Cory was still thinking about Annie maybe giving up a ride because of him as they started walking again. He glanced at her walking, facing straight ahead with a little smile on her face. He wondered how long it had been since a woman or anybody else had given up something because of him. He felt like he'd been giving up something forever.

The sun was almost straight up when they came to another gas station, this one with a sign in the window that said, "Eats."

"We might want to get something to eat," Cory said. "No telling when we'll get us another chance."

He reached into his pocket and pulled out some change and some folded-up bills and counted them.

"I've got about seven dollars and eighty cents. That ought to get us something if we don't order anything too expensive."

Annie looked at the crumpled bills in his hands. Then looked down the road, like she was trying to see where it ended.

"I don't think I could ask you to spend the last money you've got on me," she muttered. Her voice was so soft Cory couldn't tell whether she meant it or not.

"You got any money?" he asked.

"A dollar or two."

Cory jammed the bills and change back into his overall pocket and nodded.

"Then, we'll spend what we've both got."

He started walking toward the gas station until he heard Annie tell him to hold on a minute. He turned around and saw that she was pulling her shoes out of the suitcase. He stood there while she pulled them on. She tugged on the shoulder of her dress, trying to hide the tear, then she smoothed out the wrinkles.

"Alright," she said. "I'm ready."

When they entered the gas station, Cory's first thought was that these people probably made most of their money selling gas instead of food. The room was full of stacks of oil, racks of car doodads and deodorizers, and other merchandise that gas stations generally carried. There were a couple of tires leaning against the back wall.

Over on the side, there was a counter with a half dozen stools in front of it. The counter had probably been some kind of red when it was new, but now it was a dull brown, and the stools had matching plastic seats with cracks in them. On the wall behind the counter was a big picture of Jesus with a bunch of children. A strip of flypaper hung from the cord on the electric light. It looked like it had been there a while since it was pretty well covered in flies. It was a tired looking place, coated with weeks' worth of dust, and hotter inside than it was outside.

There were some hot dogs sitting on the warmer, and behind the counter, there was a woman, her back to them, scraping the grill. Her shoulders and butt shook with each scrape. Annie and Cory walked up to the counter and sat down with stools. The woman kept scraping the grill.

"Excuse me," Annie said.

The woman scraped one more scrape, then turned around and looked at them. She was an older woman—maybe 50, maybe 60—with rough hands and a rougher face. She just stared at them. Cory asked her what she had, and the woman looked around like she was hoping to see something that she had not seen before.

"You're too early for much," she said. "In a little bit, you can have pork chops and greens and some crowder peas. They're right good."

"I don't think we can wait," Annie said. "What could we have now?"

"You could have a hot dog, or I could cook you a hamburger. Can't do no French fries yet because the fryer's not working."

"How much are the hot dogs?" Cory asked.

"Fifteen cents, unless you want chili on 'em. Then they're a quarter. Have to heat up the chili, though."

Cory turned to Annie. "You want one or two hotdogs?"

"Just one." She turned to the woman. "You got any sweet tea?"

The woman nodded.

"Give us three hotdogs and two sweet teas, then," Cory said and pulled a dollar bill out of his pocket. He asked Annie if she wanted mustard and ketchup.

"That what you want on 'em?" the woman said.

Cory and Annie both nodded. The woman started putting their order together. Cory stared at the picture of Jesus behind the counter, wondering if he hadn't ought to have gone to church more. He remembered that Bible verse from Sunday School: Suffer the little children to come unto me. Cory almost laughed when he thought about suffering. He'd seen that.

When the woman had wrapped up the hot dogs, she put them in a bag and handed them to Cory, along with two big cups of sweet tea. Then she took his dollar bill and brought back his change. Annie and Cory walked back by the cans of oil and racks of deodorizers and into the sun. It seemed to be getting hotter by the minute.

They walked a little ways until they saw a clearing on the shady side of the road. There were a couple of stumps back in the shade. It looked like a good place to eat.

The hot dogs tasted rubbery, like they been on the warmer all night, but it was what they had. For several minutes they just sat on the stumps, chewing the tough hot dogs and sipping their tea.

"So you're from Albany," Cory said.

Annie shook her head, still chewing. "Not Albany. Just a little town not far from it. Town called Putney. Lived there all my life. At least so far."

"Uh-huh. What'd you do in Putney?"

"When I got out of high school, I was going to go to Albany or Tifton or someplace and get a job, maybe learn to be a secretary, but I just kept not going. I waitressed in the diner, thinking I'd go next week or next month. Then I had to go."

Cory sat there, chewing his hot dog, waiting for her to go on.

"You not going to ask me why I had to leave town?"

Cory shook his head. "I figure you'll tell me if you want to. You don't want to, you don't have to."

Annie sat up a little straighter, looking across the road at the sun-streaked woods on the other side. She wiped a bit of mustard off her mouth with her finger.

"I don't mind telling you. Fact, I'm sort of proud of it. I almost killed somebody. Not quite. But almost."

That caught Cory's attention. He couldn't figure how somebody so slight could kill somebody or almost kill them. Unless maybe they were sleeping. He just grunted.

"This boy, he kept coming to the diner. Sometimes he'd make smart remarks to me, things he'd like to do with me, but I'd been at the diner long enough that I didn't pay him no mind. Figured he was just another loudmouth.

"Then, one night I closed up the diner, and the cook left out the back door. I went out the front and locked it. I'd just gotten a little way down the block when he grabbed me and pulled me into a little alley beside a store. He was trying to get his hands under my dress, and I was fighting as hard as I could. He knocked me down and tried to get on top of me."

Annie stood up and smoothed out the skirt of her dress. She was smiling a tight smile.

"His bad luck, though. He knocked me down right beside a brick. When he leaned over, I hit him in the face with it. He fell down backward, and I crawled over and hit him again. He didn't make any noise after that."

Cory was listening so close that he had forgotten to eat his hot dog. When Annie finished, he let out a long breath.

"Sounds like you had good reason. How come you had to leave town?"

"Well, Putney had only one rich man. He owned about everything around there. That boy was his son. The boy said that I'd come on to him, then attacked him from the back, and it was all my fault. I guess the old man might have been worried that the boy's story might not do so well in court, him saying that I had hit him in the face from the back. Anyway, the old man told me that if I'd leave town and not come back, he'd get me to Albany and buy me a bus ticket to Atlanta. Since I'd been wanting to get away from there anyway, I took him up on it."

Cody looked up at the sun. It was getting up about midday, and it wasn't going to get any cooler until after dark. He put the last bite of hot dog in his mouth and put the wrapper in the paper bag.

"We probably ought to get back on the road," he said. "It's just going to get hotter, and it'd be good if we could hitch a ride."

Annie took the last swallow of her tea, then she took her shoes off and stuffed them in her suitcase.

"I'm ready when you are," she said.

They just walked along the shoulder of the road, feeling the heat radiating off the blacktop. When a car or a truck came along heading for Smithfield, Cory would stick his thumb out, but none of the cars slowed down.

"You didn't tell me about you," Annie said.

"What do you mean?"

"I told you my story. Now let's hear yours."

Cory thought about it. "Not much to it. Got born. Got married. That's it. Spent most of my life between the rows or listening to my wife tell me what I was doing wrong."

"So, you're married."

"I guess. I got a wife. Got a son, too. Neither one of them thinks a lot of me."

"I don't believe that," Annie said. "I've only known you for a little bit, but you seem like somebody I'd think a lot of."

"Maybe that's because you've only known me for a little bit. They don't, and it's gotten to the point I don't think much of me either."

"Why's that?"

They walked a little further while Cody tried to think of a good reason for Agnes and Junior not to like him or him not to like himself. Truth be told, he didn't know why, just that every morning was a new day of dealing with Agnes' disapproval and wondering why Junior didn't care.

"I don't know," he said finally. "I get up every day and go out to the fields. Sometimes Junior comes with me and does a decent day's work. I bring in a crop every year, about as good as anybody who lives around me. The bad years I've had, everybody had."

"Maybe your wife thinks you don't love her?"

Cody nodded. "That'd be about right. I guess I did sometime, but not now. She's the reason I'm here. I've been run out of my own home. Off my own land."

Annie stopped and looked at him.

"She made you leave." She looked like she was about to get mad.

"She didn't tell me to. Not in those words. But it was the way she acted."

He started to walk on, but she tugged his sleeve. He looked at her. Her head was sort of cocked to one side, and her face was scrunched up.

"Why did you marry her?"

It bothered Cory that Annie kept asking questions. For the first one, he felt like he didn't have a real good answer. This one, he probably did, but in his mind that brought up a bunch of memories that he had pushed down.

The night that he found out that he was going to marry Agnes, he'd been sitting with his mother in the kitchen, smoking a cigarette while she cleaned up the dishes. For about three years, it'd been just him and his mother. His daddy had worked himself to death farming on shares. Now Cory had taken his daddy's place, farming the little acreage for Mr. Thompson in River Falls and supporting his mother.

He heard Mr. Turner out in the yard.

"Cory Messer, I need to talk to you."

Cory's mother looked at him, and he shook his head. He didn't know what Mr. Turner wanted. He pulled himself off the chair and went to the front door.

Mr. Turner stood out in the yard. One time he'd been a big man, but consumption had hollowed him out. He was still tall, but frail-looking. He was coughing into a handkerchief. Still, he looked like a man who owned his own land; he had a good hat and a good coat.

Cory walked out onto the porch. "Hey, Mr. Turner. What can I do for you?"

"Agnes tells me she's with child, and you're the daddy."

Cory heard that at the same time he realized that Mr. Turner's hand that wasn't holding the handkerchief was holding a gun, a nasty looking over-and-under thing with two big barrels.

Mr. Turner stuffed the handkerchief back into his pocket and cradled the shotgun. "I expect you're going to do the right thing."

Cory heard his mother behind him. "That so, Cory?"

Cory was stuck between his mother and Mr. Turner, and he didn't think he could lie to either one of them.

"Yes, ma'am. It might be."

Mr. Turner took a step toward the porch, shifting the shotgun.

"What do you mean, it might be? You think my Agnes has been sleeping with all the poor white trash around here."

“No, sir. I mean, I don’t know. It might be somebody besides me.”

“She says it was you. That’s good enough for me.”

Cory’s mother moved up beside him. “I suppose that’s about right, Cory. If it could have been you, and Agnes says it was you, then I expect you’re the daddy.”

“Mama, I don’t know.”

“Cory, if she’s good enough to bed, she’s good enough to wed.” She turned to Mr. Turner. “My boy will do the right thing, Mr. Turner.”

Cory just kept looking back and forth between his mama and the man who would be his father-in-law. He didn’t understand why his mother wanted to believe Mr. Turner so quick until she explained it to him later. She wanted her boy to be more than a sharecropper, and Agnes’ daddy—her sickly daddy—owned a good piece of land, and Agnes was his only child.

That wasn’t a memory Cory liked to recall. Nor the memory of the wedding three days later in the parlor of Mr. Turner’s house. Agnes told him that she was already three months along, so they didn’t have any time to waste. A preacher came, pronounced them man and wife, took some money from Mr. Turner, and left. Cory moved into Mr. Turner’s house and started working the fields. For the rest of the year, he still had to work the fields around his mama’s house, so she could still live there. That winter, Mr. Turner died, and Cory’s mother moved into the house with them, helping take care of Junior and the house. But the next year, she died, too. She had just gone to bed and didn’t wake up. The doctor said it was probably a heart attack, and Agnes said that when she went, she wanted to go like Cory’s mother instead of like her daddy.

When his mind came back from his mama’s dying, Annie was still staring at him, waiting for an answer, her eyebrows raised just a little bit.

“Well, why did you marry her?”

"Had to. If I hadn't, her daddy would have killed me. He told me I was going to marry Agnes. I said, 'Yes, sir.'"

She just nodded and started walking again. Cory liked that he could talk to her and not be blamed for something. He knew that there were a lot of things he should be blamed for. For getting Agnes pregnant. For forgetting to put oil in their old Ford. For not going to church like he was supposed to. A man was supposed to take the blame for the things he did wrong, but what chapped Cory was being blamed for things he didn't do and couldn't do anything about. God made nematodes. God sent too much rain that made the fields muddy and the crops rot. God took Agnes' daddy and his momma. And nobody scowled at God while they scrubbed the oilcloth on the kitchen table about through. Nobody yelled at God before she stomped off and slammed the door. That was the part that Cory didn't like and couldn't understand.

He kept looking over his shoulder to see if there were any cars. There wasn't much going on either way.

Cory figured that between the gnats, the sun, and the dust kicked up by the occasional car going by that Annie had wished she'd stayed in Albany or Atlanta. But she wasn't really sweating, just walking along, a little smile on her face. Cory wished Agnes was like Annie. Just putting one foot in front of the other, not blaming or complaining. He hitched up her suitcase and walked along beside her.

"Tell me something," she said.

Cory was so far inside his own head that he almost didn't know that Annie was speaking to him.

"What?"

"What did you set out to be. Like I was going to be a secretary. Were you always going to be a farmer?

Cory thought about his brogans, his overalls, and his blue, sweat-stained shirt. They were farmer clothes, not much use for anybody else. And, except for the suit he wore to Mr. Turner's and his mama's funerals, those were the only kind of clothes he owned or needed.

"I guess so. It's about all I knew. I had to leave school when I was in the ninth grade to help my daddy. He was sickly. Then he died. I found him in the field that morning, face down in fresh-chopped dirt, still holding his hoe. After that, it was up to me to do the farming. Didn't think about anything else."

She sighed a soft sigh. "I did. Maybe it wasn't a big dream, like the girl in my class who wanted to go to Hollywood and be a movie star. But it would've gotten me out of Putney, and maybe I could have found a nice man and gotten married. I think everybody ought to have a dream, even if it's just a little one."

"You know there's a movie star that came from right around here?"

She shook her head.

"Ava Gardner. Big movie star that came from over round Smithfield." He pointed in front of them. "Eight, maybe ten miles over yonder."

"I've heard of her," Annie said. "Pretty lady. I saw her last year in a movie at the Roxy in Albany. Something about a Spanish lady. She was so pretty. The boy I was with, I don't think he closed his mouth from start to finish. He forgot I was there. Didn't make me mad. I nearly forgot he was there, too. Miss Gardner was so pretty."

Annie flashed a smile at him.

"If pretty is what it takes to get you to Hollywood, I guess I better keep on walking."

"You're pretty enough," Cory said. He was comparing her to Agnes. He guessed that he'd thought Agnes was pretty one time. She'd had eyes that had started smiling before her mouth did. And sometimes they looked like they were looking right into him, knowing what he was thinking. He remembered sitting on the bank of the creek that ran between their farms and just looking at her eyes. He held her hand, and their feet dangled in the cool water. He didn't remember what they'd talked about.

Cory and Annie fell silent again. He was thinking about Agnes fifteen years ago before Mr. Turned came to his house with the shotgun. Then Junior had been born six months after they got married, and all the old ladies were counting on their fingers, but Agnes didn't seem to care. Her daddy was sick. She had a husband and a new baby to take care of. She said she didn't have time to worry about what a bunch of old biddies were saying. She'd laugh and tell him she didn't need anything from them.

Then her daddy died, and Junior got older. There were some bad years, and they'd sold off a few acres. It bothered Agnes a lot when they sold the land. She said it was like they were getting rid of a piece of her daddy. That's when the smile had gone out of her eyes, and her laugh just disappeared. They didn't come back. That was when she started to pull back from him. Between being in the fields all day and being tired at night, he didn't notice it at first. Then after the crops were in and the days got shorter, he could see it. He'd reach for her hand, and she'd get up and start to do something. Or he'd kiss her, and she'd turn her head; he would kiss her cheek. She didn't kiss him back.

She'd said she was busy with Junior. He'd just started walking, and all she had time for was to cook dinner, clean house, and keep up with him. First, he said he understood. Then, after months, he understood something else. She was using all of that to keep away from him. There was this blanket of blame that seemed to lay over the whole house. It seemed like the only thing that gave Agnes pleasure was finding fault with him. Cory felt like he was being pushed face-first into a wall, not able to do a bit better.

He saw a little house just up the road.

"If you're thirsty, I bet we can get some water here. Most folks around here don't mind."

"That'd be good. Maybe I should have saved some of that sweet tea."

As soon as Cory stepped into the yard, he felt smaller, about ten or eleven years old, a time when he lived in a house just like this and kept living there until he married Agnes. The clean, swept yard was the same. The little house was unpainted; the whitest thing about it was the refrigerator sitting on the front porch.

Cory knew what the inside looked like. A bigger room for cooking and sitting and a couple of smaller rooms for sleeping. Around back, there would be a well or a pump, an outhouse, and probably some chickens. He remembered getting off the school bus just down the road from his house, hoping that his classmates who lived in bigger houses painted white and had indoor plumbing couldn't see where he lived. But they all knew. He knew that.

He didn't see anybody around, but when they got into the yard, he heard a voice.

"Something I can do for y'all?"

The voice was followed by an old colored man walking around the corner of the house, a sturdy-looking man despite his gray hair and a limp that caused his left foot to drag the ground.

"I didn't know if there's anyone here," Cory said.

"Uh-huh. When I see somebody coming, I usually go inside or around the corner of the house. There's some boys around who think it's fun to mess with an old man, throw things at him from their car. Last year I got hit with a Coca-Cola bottle. Bout broke my shoulder and took me about a month before I could do anything with that arm. Y'all walking?"

Cory nodded. "I guess. Been trying to hitch a ride all morning, but ain't had no luck yet."

The old man nodded. “Guess everybody’s just in a hurry to get where they’re going.” He nodded to Annie. “Ma’am, you don’t look like you’re dressed for a long walk.”

Annie laughed. “No, I didn’t plan on walking so far. I guess it’s just the way it is.”

“Wonder if we could trouble you for some water?” Cory asked.

“Ain’t no trouble. Got a pump and a dipper right around back. Good, cool well water.”

He started walking around the corner of the house, Cory and Annie following. Cory saw the chicken yard at the back of the property and an old pickup sitting beside a shed. At the house, on a small square of a back porch, there was a bench with a pump on it. Just over it, hanging on a nail, was a dipper.

“My name’s Romie,” the old man said, nodding to Annie and Cory.

“I’m Cory, and this is Annie. Pleased to meet you.”

Romie pulled the dipper from the nail and leaned on the pump handle. After a couple of pumps, the water started pouring into the dipper. Romie looked at Cory, then threw the water out and filled up the dipper again. He handed it to Annie, and she took a long swallow.

“Thank you, Romie. That’s good.”

The two men watched as Annie finished drinking the water. Then she handed the dipper to Cory.

He filled it, drank it, and filled it again. Then he wiped his mouth on the back of his hand.

“That was good. Thank you.”

Romie grinned. “One thing I got is good, cold well water. You’re welcome to more if you want it.”

Cory shook his head, then pointed to the pickup.

“No, thank you. But I wonder if I could talk you into giving us a ride into Smithfield. Be too much trouble?”

"Wouldn't be no trouble at all if it'd run. Needs a new fuel pump. I've been saving up for it, but it's taking a while. You know how farming is."

Cody nodded. He didn't tell Romie that he sure did. That's why he was walking away from it. He just said that he understood.

"I guess it's about as bad as any job in the world, but I wouldn't do nothing else," Romie said.

"Why's that?" Annie asked.

Romie pointed toward a little path that ran between some trees.

"Right down there, I got me a garden. Sweet corn. Peas. Peppers. Butter beans. Always got something to eat. And over there, I got about an acre and a quarter of tobacco. I can still get it in, what with my neighbor's help. I help them. They help me. Plenty to eat. A little money."

"What about the bad years. No money. Some people lose their land," Cory said, maybe a little sharper than he meant to. Romie's idea of farming wasn't matching up with what he'd told Annie.

"That's true. There's bad years, and I've seen some. But then there's always next year. That's one thing I learned. I've been doing this more than 70 years, and no matter how bad this year is, there's always a next one."

"Yep, I suppose there is. Thank you for the water. We best get back on the road. Might be able to hitch a ride." He looked at the path going between the trees. "This your land?"

Romie nodded. "Been mine for a long time. My wife and I bought it in 1932. Mr. Fanning, a real nice white man I'd been farming for on shares, told me he wanted me to have a farm of my own. So we made a deal that the farm would be mine, and his share would go for payments. Took a while, but we bought it. Raised a boy here. He's off working in Raleigh now, but I think he'll be back. It'll be his land then."

Cody just nodded his head and looked around for Annie.

She was running some water over her hands and then her face. She leaned over and wiped her face with the edge of her skirt. Cory saw the lacy hem of her slip.

"I'm looking forward to getting to Smithfield," she said. "I want to see where Ava Gardner came from."

Romie's face lit up as if someone had switched on the light. "Miss Ava? She ain't from Smithfield. She's from Grabtown."

"I thought she was from Smithfield," Cory said.

"Most folks think that. Mostly because nobody knows about Grabtown."

"That's a fact," Cory said. "I've lived over by River Falls all my life, and I never heard of it."

"Ain't much to know about Grabtown. Just a wide spot in the road with a couple of stores. Used to have a post office, but it got closed. Grabtown's just two or three miles up the road."

"Do you know where Ava Gardner's house was? That's what I want to see," Annie said.

Romie grinned and nodded his head. "It's right off this road. Fact, you can see it from the highway. I used to work some with Miss Ava's daddy. She was always running around. Almost never had on any shoes."

"You think she always wanted to be a movie star?" Annie asked.

Romie scratched his gray head. "Never heard her talk of it. But I figured she was going to something instead of marrying some sharecropper and staying home and raising babies. Her and her sister, too."

Cory had been edging toward the front of the house, trying to catch Annie's eye, but she was still talking to Romie. Looked like the old black man was enjoying having some company. Finally, he walked over and tapped Annie on the shoulder.

"Annie, we best be getting on if we want to make to it Smithfield by dark."

She nodded. "Thank you for the water and the information, Romie. You were very kind." She patted him on the arm.

"Wasn't no trouble," he said. "Hope y'all get a ride. It's too hot to be walking now."

"It is," Annie said. "But tell me. How will we know when we get to Ava Gardner's house?"

"It's got a little sign. When her daddy died, somebody from Smithfield bought the house and was going to fix it into a museum, but I hear that all he's done yet is put up a little sign on the road."

"We'll watch out for the sign," Cory said, pulling on Annie's elbow. Romie turned to hang the dipper back on its nail, and Annie and Cory walked around the corner of the house back to the road.

"He's a nice man," Annie said.

"Some coloreds are real nice. Some not so nice."

Annie was quiet while she processed what Cory had said. Then she nodded.

"About like everybody else, then."

"You don't have any coloreds down in Putney, Georgia?"

"Not many. We had some out in the country, and there were a bunch of them over in Albany, but there wasn't much for them to do in Putney. Not many places where they were welcome."

Cory hitched up Annie's suitcase, and they walked along the edge of the road. He kept looking over his shoulder for a car heading toward Smithfield.

Suddenly, Cory heard a loud car behind them and a yell. He turned around in time to see something coming from the car. He pushed Annie back and stepped in front of her. She stumbled, and he felt something graze his hip. It clattered along the side of the road and came to rest at the edge of the blacktop. It was an empty beer can.

"You okay?" he asked Annie.

She nodded. "That was a brave thing for you to do," she said.

Cory was checking his overalls to see if they been torn. He couldn't tell where the beer can hit him.

"Nah, it was just an empty beer can."

"But you didn't know that. That was about the bravest thing anybody's ever done for me." She was staring at him with her eyes wide, like she wondered how she could be next to a person like him. Cory started to dismiss it again but didn't. If she wanted to think he was brave, he'd let her think that. It felt so good he puffed up his chest a bit.

"I reckon those were some of the boys Romie was talking about," she said.

"Likely."

They walked along, not talking much as the sun got hotter and hotter. Cory pulled out his handkerchief and wiped his face. He started to offer it to Annie but thought better of it. She wasn't sweating much anyway. After about an hour, they saw a little sign that said, "Ava Gardner's Childhood Home." An arrow pointed to a little two-track lane that led off the highway.

Cory looked at the shadows getting longer and wondered if they ought to head on to Smithfield. Hot as it was, the days weren't real long yet, and he didn't want them walking down the highway in the dark. He mentioned that to Annie.

"You mean you don't want to see where a real movie star grew up? I do. And this may be the only chance I ever get. Romie said it was just a little ways down the road."

Cory didn't have the heart to argue. He didn't care whether he saw where a real movie star grew up or not; it wouldn't change anything about his life. But seeing Annie excited and happy made him feel better, so he just nodded, and they turned down the path.

The house at the end of the path wasn't a whole lot different from any other house along that road. This one was painted white, and it didn't have a refrigerator on the front porch. There were a couple of rocking chairs at one end of the porch and a swing at the other. The yard had been swept, and there wasn't any trash lying around. Somebody was keeping the house up.

Cory walked up on the porch and knocked on the door. He didn't hear anything from inside the house, so he knocked again.

"Don't think there's anybody here," he said. Annie was standing in the yard, looking at the house. She walked up on the porch and knocked on the front door. Her knock sounded small compared to Cory's. There still was no sound from inside.

"Nope. Guess not," she said. Then she turned the doorknob, and the front door opened. "But they left the front door unlocked for us."

Cory took a couple of steps back. "I don't know if we ought to go in there," he said. "Round here, you can get shot for going in somebody's house."

Annie pushed the door open and walked across the threshold, looking around.

"But this isn't just somebody's house. This is Ava Gardner's. And they can't expect us to walk all this way and not at least look around. Besides, I bet nobody's coming back."

Cory figured that was true. It must be over toward five o'clock, and this would be a chance to get out of the sun for a little while anyway. He stepped inside the house and put Annie's suitcase beside the front door.

They were in the front room of the house. It looked like it had been lived in, but whoever lived in it quit fifteen or twenty years ago. The furniture must have been just like it was when Ava Gardner lived there. The big overstuffed sofa had flattened and worn cushions. Next to it was an oak table with a fringe-shaded lamp. On the other side of the table was a blue high-backed chair that looked too fancy for the rest of the furniture. A single electric bulb hung from the ceiling in the middle of the room, and a rag rug covered most of the floor. It had probably been bright colors years ago, but now it was faded to almost no colors at all.

"I bet Ava Gardner sat on that sofa," Annie said. She had her hands clasped in front of her and looked like she was about to start jumping up and down. She started turning slowly, noting each of the three doors that led off the parlor.

"Let's go in there," she said, pointing to the door that went to the back of the house.

It opened into the kitchen. The floor was covered with worn linoleum, worn more in front of the kerosene stove and the sink. A pump stood up at one end of the sink. On the far wall, beside the door that opened to the back porch, there was a metal cupboard. In the middle of the room, there was a table with a faded piece of oilcloth stretched across the top and two chairs and a bench beside it.

Being in the kitchen reminded Cory that he hadn't eaten since the hot dogs that morning. Somehow, walking along with Annie, he hadn't thought about how empty his stomach was.

"Wonder if they left any food in this place," he said. He figured that as empty as he was, he could get over taking something that wasn't his. He went over to the cupboard and started opening doors. There was nothing behind the first two doors, but behind the third one was three large cans of pork and beans, probably lunch for whoever worked at Ava Gardner's Childhood Home.

"You like cold beans?" he asked, holding out the can for Annie to see.

“I guess right now, I’d like most anything. But I wonder if they don’t have some kerosene in that stove. We might could warm them up.”

That didn’t feel right to Cory, but he couldn’t say why he didn’t have a problem taking somebody’s pork and beans but was uncomfortable using their stove. That didn’t make sense, so he pulled the fuel jar out of its holder; it had several inches of kerosene in it. Annie had pulled a pot from the cabinet and a can opener from a drawer. She was busy opening the beans.

Cory shrugged, pulled some matches out of his pocket, and lit the stove.

“Wonder what else they have to eat here,” Annie said. “I’m about to starve. I guess one good thing about waitressing in that diner was that I ate pretty good.” She was opening one cupboard door after another. In the lower section, she found part of a loaf of white bread. She also found some plates and glasses.

“Looks like we have everything we need for a hot dinner,” she said.

“Yep,” Cory said. “I just hope whoever this belongs to don’t get back before we leave.”

“I bet they’re gone for the day. But the bread’s fresh, so they’ve been here. Would’ve been nice if they had left us some pork chops or maybe a few slices of ham.”

“I guess we need to be grateful for what we got,” Cory said, maybe a little harsher than he meant to.

“Annie looked very serious. She clasped her hands in front of her and raised her eyes to the ceiling.

“Thank you, Ava,” she said.

Annie spooned the warm beans on the plates and took them to the table. Cory pumped some water into the glasses. Then they sat down. Most of his life, Cory or somebody had said grace before food, but he didn’t know how Annie would feel about that, so he just took a piece of bread and started eating.

They ate without talking, pushing the beans onto the fork with the white bread. When finished eating, Cory wiped the sauce from his plate with the last of a piece of bread.

"I don't guess they left any cake or pie, did they?" Cory said, grinning at Annie. He didn't feel so bad about taking or cooking the beans. He was having a strange feeling. He was content, not anxious to leave the table and the people there, but willing to just sit. He wondered if this is what other people felt like after they ate. He didn't move until Annie got up and started taking up the plates.

By the time they'd cleaned up the kitchen, the sun had gone down, and the woods across the field in the back of the house were beginning to disappear. Cory stood at the window, staring at the woods. He didn't want them to be on the road after dark. Those boys might come back and try to do something more than throw an empty beer can. And he sure didn't want to sleep in the woods.

Cory wondered how it would be to be married to a woman like Annie, one who smiled and got excited about Ava Gardner's house. He tried to remember when Agnes got excited—in a good way—about anything.

Annie left, maybe to go to the outhouse. Cory just stood there, staring at the dark shapes of the tops of the trees. He remembered before Junior was born, Agnes' belly was getting bigger every day. One night after dinner, they walked down to the pond. He was holding her hand.

While they were walking, Agnes laughed out loud. He didn't know what at; he hadn't said anything.

Then she put his hand on her belly and laughed again. "Can you really want to be around a woman with a belly like this?" she said. Cory didn't know what to say, so he just pulled her close to him and kissed her. It was the only answer he had. One of the things that he remembered most was that she kissed him back. He felt his eyes get moist, and he wiped them with his fingers.

Annie came back in through the back door. He asked her if there was any paper in the outhouse.

"Yeah. I guess somebody must work here during the day or something. They got all the comforts of home."

"That's good. Because it looks like we'll be here for the night anyway. I think I'll go see the outhouse for myself."

"You think it's a good idea to stay here. I mean, I imagine somebody'll be here in the morning. We might be in trouble."

Cory noticed that Annie sounded a little like Agnes. But instead of thinking it was a quarreling sound, he thought it was a scared sound. She was scared of being caught, and they might be. They could be arrested for trespassing, or if whoever showed up had a gun, they might be shot. It was a problem worth pondering, but he didn't want to ponder it in front of Annie.

"We just need to make sure we leave before they get here. Probably it's just an old maid lady anyway, wanting to do something for Ava." He started toward the back door, then turned to her. "I don't think you want to sleep in the woods. I know I don't. You say there was some paper in the outhouse?"

She nodded, and he went out back.

Later in the evening, they were in the sitting room, Annie on the sofa and Cory in the high-back chair. The small square room looked a lot better in the light of the lamp. The rag rug on the floor didn't look so faded, and the walls, going to darkness at the edge of the lamplight, didn't show the flaking paint.

"Tell me about your wife," Annie said.

"What do you mean?"

"Well, tell me if she's big or little. Or if her hair is black or brown or maybe—after being married to you—it's gone gray." She grinned to let him know she was teasing. "I just want to know something about where you came from. Maybe why you're so willing to leave it."

Cory thought about it for a bit. Putting things into words wasn't something he did real well, especially when it didn't involve crops or stock. Finally, something struck him.

"She's got more education than I do. She finished high school. Said one time she wanted to go to college to be a teacher. She could've, too. Her daddy had the money. He'd give her anything she wanted. She read a lot, not so much now, but right after we got married, she still read a whole lot of books, and sometimes she'd tell me about them. Most of what I know about books is from what she told me.

"She was just a girl when we got married, but she was a pretty one. I'd of married her, even if I hadn't had to. She made me feel good to be around her."

Annie tucked her bare feet up under her on the sofa.

"So far, I don't see so much to run away from."

"I'm not running away. I'm just leaving. All that was years ago. It's changed some now. It's changed a lot."

"Is she still pretty?"

"I guess so. If you didn't know what she was thinking, you'd think she was pretty. But I do. I know what she's thinking every day. Hard to see her as pretty when she's thinking that there's not much to you."

"I guess so. So, she doesn't think much of you, and you don't think much of her, and your boy takes her side. I can see how that might be hard to live with."

Then the conversation wandered off onto other subjects. Cory's farm. Annie's job, how long Ava Gardner had been gone from this house. Then it dribbled into silence. He thought Annie might be going to sleep, but, abruptly, she sat up.

"I don't believe you," she said.

Cory roused himself out of the half-sleep he'd drifted into.

“What? What don’t you believe?”

“I don’t believe that you don’t have some kind of dream. Like I wanted to be a secretary. And Agnes wanted to be a schoolteacher. I bet you that your son has his own dream if you asked him. I think everybody should have some sort of dream.”

Cory yawned, raised his arms over his head to stretch, and wriggled in the high-back chair.

“You don’t know much about farming, do you?”

Annie shook her head. “Not much. I’ve always lived in town, but no place in Putney is more than a half-mile from somebody’s farm.”

“It ain’t how close you are to a farm; it’s if you worked it. If you’re working a farm, there’s not a lot of time for looking far out. Sometimes you don’t look further than the end of the day. Sometimes you don’t look further than the end of the row.”

He sat forward, realizing he was putting something into words that he knew but had never said.

“On the farm, there are things you have to do every season and at certain times during that season. You know, when they say in the Bible that there’s a time to plant and a time to gather, they meant it. That’s what we do.

“If you’ve got some stock, there’s things you have to do every day. You don’t get to pick when you do things. So I get up in the morning, and I know what has to be done. I go out and do it.” His voice was getting louder as he talked. He leaned toward her. “And since I was a boy, that’s what I did. Every day. Every damn day.”

Annie brought her hands up to her face. “I’m sorry,” she said. “I didn’t mean to make you feel bad. I’ll just shut up.”

Cory hauled himself out of the blue chair and walked over to the window. He had just realized that his whole life—boy and man—he’d been doing the next thing he was supposed to do. He’d heard the preacher talk about free will, but for the life of him, he couldn’t figure out where his was.

He could see the glow of some car lights on the highway, people all going somewhere. He turned back to Annie.

"It wasn't what you said. I think it was that this is the first time I ever thought of it that way. I started farming when I was little, round the tobacco barn when I was seven or eight. By the time I was sixteen, my daddy got sick, and I quit school. That didn't matter much because I'd missed a lot of school helping Daddy. But I was sixteen, and I felt like a man, doing a man's work."

He turned back around to the window, trying to see the lights. When he spoke again, it was like he was talking to himself.

"Now, I'm thirty-five, and I don't feel like a man. I don't know what I feel like. It feels like Agnes and Junior and those rows of tobacco and corn have sucked the manhood right out of me. All I know is that I got up this morning and decided that I wasn't going to be doing that anymore. Or feeling like that anymore."

Annie walked up behind him and put her hand on his shoulder. He shivered a little bit when he felt it.

"And how do you feel now?" she asked.

He shook his head slowly, hoping she wouldn't take her hand off his shoulder.

"I don't know. About the same. Maybe it's too soon to tell."

She took her hand off his shoulder and stepped up beside him, looking out the window into the dark.

"So maybe you brought Agnes and Junior and all those rows of tobacco with you." She patted his arm. "Maybe we ought to get some sleep if we're going to get up early enough not to get caught. There may be something in the icebox we can eat for breakfast, too."

"Whoever wakes up first needs to wake up the other one," Cory said.

"Uh-huh. Probably ought to be gone by the time it gets light. I'd hate for the first thing I see in Smithfield to be the jail."

She picked up her suitcase and headed back toward the bedroom. Then she turned around and came back, looking right into his face.

"You're a good man, Cory. Don't let anybody tell you any different. I'm glad we met up. You've already done more for me than almost anybody. I appreciate that."

Cory turned around to face her. His chest felt full, but he wasn't going to tear up in front of Annie.

"It's nice of you to say so, Annie," he said. "I don't see that it was that much, but I'm glad it helped. Hope you can get some sleep."

"You, too," she said and went into the bedroom.

Cory just stared out the window, watching the car lights going both ways. Maybe Annie was right; wherever he went, Agnes and Junior and the crops were with him. He wondered if that was the way it was supposed to be, and if it was, why did it feel so bad. He remembered the feel of Annie's hand on his shoulder, how good that felt.

Next door to the bedroom Annie was using was another one, smaller, with two little cots instead of a real bed, but Cory figured it would be enough for him. He heard Annie leave the bedroom to go to the kitchen. He figured she was washing up before bed. That'd be a good thing to do, but he'd wait until he heard her go back into the bedroom.

After washing up and taking off his brogans, overalls, and shirt, Cory stretched out on the cot, feeling the weariness ease out of his legs. It wasn't a bad place to be, no worse than staring at the closed door of his and Agnes' bedroom when she'd stomped off and slammed it. He couldn't remember what they had been arguing about. He just remembered it had been loud. At least, it was quiet here.

He had to turn over two or three times before he could really get comfortable, but finally, the quiet and the fatigue of the day came over him, and he slept until he heard a noise beyond the closed door. He pulled on his overalls and ran into the parlor.

It was still dark there, but there was a light in the kitchen. He peered in and saw Annie standing at the kerosene stove, turning something in the frying pan. She had on a different dress. This one was clean and probably wasn't torn.

"Good morning," he said. "You found us something to eat. That's good."

"Don't get your hopes up. All I could find was the rest of that loaf of white bread. I'm making us some toast. They don't have any coffee, but there was a soft drink in the icebox. So we got something to eat and something to wash it down with."

"Better'n nothing. I'll go get my clothes on."

Cory went back to the bedroom and finished dressing. He thought about how calm Annie looked, flipping the toast made of some stranger's stolen bread in a kitchen they weren't supposed to be in. Seemed that that calmness was catching, that he didn't have the churning in his stomach that he'd had when he started walking away from home. The corners of his lips turned up into a smile. Calmness felt good.

When he got back into the kitchen, Annie had set the table with two pieces of toast each and a glass full of some kind of soft drink. They sat silently, chewing on the dry toast and washing it with the drink.

"Do you believe in ghosts?"

Cory's head jerked up. He was sure he had misunderstood her. She saw the puzzled look on his face and repeated the question.

"Do you believe in ghosts?"

He'd heard her right the first time. Seemed like a strange way to start a conversation first thing in the morning. A long way from "did you sleep good?"

"I don't think so. When I was a kid, I believed in ghosts, I guess. Daddy used to tell a lot of ghost stories. For a while, I was afraid to go out to the outhouse at night. But daddy liked to fool around a lot. I got to where I didn't believe in them. What made you ask about ghosts?"

Annie looked down at her plate, slowly chewing her toast, probably more times than the piece of bread needed.

"Because one came to me last night. It was Ava Gardner."

"I'm pretty sure she's not dead," Cory said. "If she'd died, somebody would have said something about it. She's right famous around here."

Annie's face was all scrunched up like she was thinking hard. Then she shook her head.

"I don't know about that. I just woke up in the middle of the night, and there she was, big as life. She had on such a pretty dress and a big string of pearls, but she was barefooted. She had this sort of smile on her face, like she knew something I didn't know. And she just stood there."

"Did she talk to you?"

"She did. And she used a lot of really ugly words. But not in a bad way. She said since I was there, sleeping in her mama and daddy's bed, she figured she'd help me out."

"What did you say?" Cory asked. He was torn between talking about this ghost and wanting to talk about something he thought was more usual.

"I didn't say anything. She just went on talking. She said that I ought to stop being so afraid. Sort of like the angel that showed up when Jesus was born. Don't be afraid. I didn't know what she was talking about, but I couldn't say anything. I was afraid. I've never seen a ghost before. Then she said she wasn't talking about being afraid of some a—she used some words here I don't use—ghost. She was talking about being afraid of stepping out into life.

"She said if she'd been as afraid as I was, she'd still be in Smithfield living on the edge of a tobacco field with a bunch of little'uns running around. She said she wasn't afraid, and she'd gone to Hollywood, and she'd married a bunch of famous people like Frank Sinatra and Mickey Rooney, and she'd kissed Humphrey Bogart, and she'd been all over the world. So, she told me I should quit being afraid and not to just settle for some job just because I needed a job, but to go after what I really wanted. She said it would be fine if I would do that."

"Yeah," Cory said. "You should get yourself a good job. That sounds like good advice. It'd be good for you to be doing something you really want to do, not what you've always been doing."

Annie sat there for a minute. She had finished her toast, so she just twisted her fingers like she was trying to wind herself up to do something.

"She told me to tell you something, too," she said. "I don't know why she didn't want to tell you herself, I mean since it seems she can get around so easy. She said to tell the man in the next bedroom to quit worrying so much about what other people think."

"I don't know what that means," he said.

"Yeah, she said you'd say something like that, so she told me to tell you that it means that your character is determined by what you do, not by what others do to you. That's what she said. Course she used some words I don't use."

Cory just nodded. He didn't know how he felt taking advice from a ghost through a stranded woman he just met. What did Ava Garner know about Cory Messer, anyway? For that matter, what did she know about Annie? And how did she get to be a ghost and a movie star at the same time?

Cory stared down at his empty plate. He'd been glad that Annie was going to step out and do what she wanted, whether it was because of Ava Gardner's advice or not. Sometimes people just needed to do something brave.

"I hope you take Ava Gardner's advice, Annie," Cory said. "You deserve something good, and I hope you get it."

He picked up his plate and took it to the sink, pumping some water over it and wiping it with a dishrag that was hanging there. He started to put it in the cabinet but put it back on the table instead. He pulled out the crumpled-up dollar bills. He had six dollars left. Cory smoothed out three of them and put them beside the plate.

"You're a good man, Cory. I said it last night, and you just showed you were again," she said, nodding to the three dollar bills. "Lots of people do good when everybody knows about it. Takes somebody special to do good when nobody's going to know who did it."

Cory shrugged.

"Just don't feel right to eat somebody else's food. Not when I don't have to."

"There's something else."

"Ava Gardner told you something else?"

"No," she said. "This is just me. You said I deserve something good. I think I do. But I think you do, too. I think you deserve something real good."

They finished cleaning up the kitchen, and Annie went to get her suitcase out of the bedroom. Cory walked around the house, making sure that they had put everything back where it belonged. Ava Gardner had given them a decent night's shelter. It was right to leave it like they found it.

He noticed a little book on the shelf under the parlor table. It must've been there the night before, but he hadn't seen it. He picked it up and settled back on the sofa, sinking into it. The book looked like some sort of diary, although it didn't have a lock on it. He opened it, looking at the words written in pencil in a large schoolgirl script.

"My name is Ava. One day a lot of people are going to know that. My daddy says that there's a whole lot more world out there than Grabtown, but he never got to see it. He wants my sister and me to see it, and we will."

He flipped to the next page and read about where she had gone to the moving pictures and how pretty the women were. Then he turned to the back of the book. By the time she wrote that, she evidently had gotten older. The handwriting was smaller and neater. It was a short entry, the very last one. It said, "Daddy told me today that sitting around and dreaming was never going to get me what I want. I can't leave here yet, but maybe next year, I'll take the first step. I don't know what it'll be or how it'll turn out."

Cory thought about Ava Gardner sitting on the sofa or maybe on the cot in her room, trying to figure out what she was going to do. That day or maybe a few days later, she had set her eyes on something. Turned out that she had done it. That was good.

He put the little book back under the table, waiting for Annie to come out of the bedroom. It struck him that he'd never set his eyes on anything but what was right in front of him. He'd worked his daddy's share of the farm, he'd gotten married, and he'd planted and harvested every year, but he never set his eyes further out than this crop and maybe the next one.

Ava Garner had charged through life. She might have been too poor to have shoes, but when she got rich, she still went barefoot. Probably a lot of people in Grabtown, what people there were in this little place, laughed at her, figured she was putting on airs, but she went out to Hollywood and became a movie star. It was a world bigger than Grabtown. She must've been some woman.

What was it Annie said Ava had told her? That other people don't make you what you are. Cory wondered what that was, something more than somebody stooping between the rows.

He'd been a faithful husband for more than fifteen years. He'd tried to be a good father, even if Junior didn't think so now. And he knew he was a good farmer. Not every year was a good one, but when good years came, they prospered.

Annie came into the parlor, carrying her suitcase.

"Do you think it's early enough? I don't want us getting caught, even if you did leave money for the food."

Cory looked out the window. It was just getting light enough to see across the field next to the house.

"I imagine. Looks like it's just a little bit after six. I don't think anybody is going to come here this early. We'll just walk on, and they'll never know we've been here."

Annie laughed.

"They probably will, but they won't know who it was. That's good enough for me."

They walked out the front door, making sure it was closed behind them, and down the path leading to the highway. Smithfield wasn't that far off, just a few miles, and they would have finished their journey. As they walked, Annie still barefoot in the cool morning, it struck Cory that maybe now was the time to set his eyes on something.

There had been bad years, but there had also been good years. There was the anger of Agnes, but there was also the Agnes that he had loved. And there was Junior, who either didn't understand what the land was or didn't care, but Junior wasn't fully formed.

As they walked along the side of the highway, Cory got deeper and deeper into his head, thinking so hard that he forgot to stick out his thumb when a car going to Smithfield passed them. Annie didn't say anything about it.

Then an old Chevrolet pulled up in front of them. Cory walked up to the window. Inside was somebody about Cory's daddy's age, mostly bald with gray around his head. He smiled at Cory.

"Just wondered if you folks might need a lift. Noticed that you had a suitcase, so I figured you weren't just out for a stroll," he said.

"You're right. A ride to Smithfield would be real nice if that's where you're going."

Cory opened the passenger door and put Annie's bag in the back seat. He left it open when he walked around to the driver's side.

"The lady there is Annie," Cory said.

The man nodded. "I'm Claude."

"Annie's had a bad time lately," Cory said, speaking softly so that Annie couldn't hear him. "I've been trying to help a little. I hope you'll make sure she gets to Smithfield safe, and if there's something you can do to help her meet some people, I'd appreciate it."

Claude nodded, glancing at Annie, who was still standing at the passenger door.

"None of my business, I guess, but is she a relative?"

"Nope. I just met her yesterday. She seems like a good woman, somebody who would make a fine secretary or something like that."

Claude just looked at him for a minute. Then he nodded again.

Cory walked back around the car and motioned for Annie to get in the front seat.

"Where are you going to be, Cory?" For the second time since they had been together, Cory heard some fear in her voice.

"I'll be doing something, I guess. Not in Smithfield. This man's name is Claude, and I think you'll be safe with him and maybe he can help you get situated. Go with him. I hope you the best."

Annie hesitated before getting into the car. Cory pushed the door closed, gave Claude a little salute, and smiled at Annie. The car slowly pulled back onto the blacktop and then picked up speed. Cory watched it until it disappeared around the curve.

Cory took a deep breath and turned back toward River Falls. He started walking, putting one scarred brown brogan after another, with his shoulders back and his back straight.

The World Beyond the Window

PROLOGUE

I can't claim to be wise. I'm only twenty-four, and I think it takes a lot longer than that to accumulate wisdom. I do know a lot more about comma splices, dangling participles, and subject-verb agreement than the high school students I teach, but that's just education. Hopefully, they'll know the basics of English grammar by the time they graduate; then, they'll sound like they have an education.

Wisdom is another thing entirely. You don't get it from a book. And–at least in my short experience–it doesn't come without pain. And, unless you're some kind of genius, you don't get it all by yourself.

There are a few things that I've learned that might be the beginnings of wisdom:

If, as they say, life is a journey, you shouldn't expect to end up in the same place you started. That can be either a good thing or a bad one.

We are developed not just by our own experiences but also by the experiences of other people. Life isn't really a straight line; it's more like a cobweb. In fact, if it wasn't for some other people's experiences, some of them terrible, I wouldn't be trying to convince Teddy Sommers that every paragraph needs a topic sentence and that "him and I" will probably cost him a job one of these days. If I was anything at all, I'd be stuck in the mountains, married too young, and never knowing what was on the other side of the ridge.

And, finally, love is not overrated. Real love is everything it's cracked up to be. It's the difference between shivering in your bed at night, afraid you're going to disappear completely, and feeling secure enough to get a good night's sleep. It's the difference between waking up to dread and waking up to a world that has possibilities. For me, it may have been the difference between life and death. Or a life that was worse than death.

That's the reason I'm spending this summer week by myself in a little cabin in the mountains, staring through the window at the green growth, beautiful at someplace near the midpoint between the new birth of spring and its flaming end in the fall. It's cool and crisp here, a perfect place to sit and think. I came here to remember the two women–and me. We all had stories that started differently, and just because the two women are no longer with us, they still don't end. I hope I pass some of what they knew, what they did, and what they believed to somebody else, and when I'm no longer here, the stories will just keep going on.

Because it's like a cobweb, there's no place you can say, "this is where the story starts or this is where it ends." But the best place for me to start is with Erin.

ERIN

There is, in the moments right after you have been told you're going to die, a sudden vacuum, a feeling that the world has been pulled out from under you and that you're suspended over nothingness. It's not like Wiley Coyote and the cliff, where you flail and fall anyway. It's simply space and no movement. And a gasp because something has sucked all of the air out of the room.

In an instant, I had become an object, not someone who made things happen, but someone things happened to. It was literally the first day of the end of my life. But if this story were just about dying, it would hardly be worth the telling. We all die. The method varies, and the time it takes. But just dying makes a poor story.

About the best thing that can be said about it was what Daddy said when he took me to see Hamlet. At the end of the play, when the curtain was about to go down, and everybody was lying on the floor dead, he looked at me and said, "Well, it's not a comedy."

This part of my story started in a small office on the fourteenth floor of a medical building in Atlanta. The walls were drab, almost green, and the drabness was broken by exactly fourteen frames, six with diplomas and certificates in them, the rest with pictures of Dr. Belzear and other people. And I had been waiting for nearly half an hour, fidgeting, pulling at the hem of my skirt, knowing that I had things to do at my own office, an office that was larger than his. I thought about the deadlines facing me when I got back, scheduling the rest of my day in my head. Then he came in and told me.

Dr. Belzear was a small, balding man. He moved in quick jerks as if he always had to be somewhere else, but when he sat down behind his desk, he was very still. He stared a moment at the file in front of him. Then he told me.

I had no frame of reference. I knew what death was, but I didn't know how to think about my own, and now this white-coated man on the other side of the desk sat there, a sad smile on his face. Dr. Belzear leaned forward, listening for me to say something.

"Are you sure?" I finally asked, the words coming out on their own while my body kept reaching for something more substantial than the space.

"I'm afraid so," he said. "I think you'll have another six to nine months, and with chemotherapy, we may be able to stretch it further—a year or more. But there's no doubt about the cancer. Or what kind it is. I'm sorry."

Dr. Belzear asked me to make an appointment with his nurse so that we could begin chemotherapy. On his way out, he stopped, probably trying to think of something to say. Then he patted me on the shoulder and left me alone in the room.

I stared at the fourteen frames on the wall and replayed our conversation. It seemed that my choice was to live six or nine months or—by taking medicine that would keep me nauseated and make my hair fall out—live maybe a year. My grandfather had had chemo, and he'd lasted a little over a year, but it was the most miserable year of his life. I was in high school, and I tried to visit him about every day, but all he could do was sit in his recliner unless he had to go into the bathroom to throw up. I had quit visiting, except when I went with Daddy. In the last weeks, he could no longer make it to the bathroom. The hospice nurse kept a pail behind his recliner. He was pale, his eyes sunken deep into their sockets, and he still hurt. He was alive, but barely. That's something I couldn't do.

I got up and left the office. The woman at the desk she asked me if I needed to make another appointment. I just shook my head. I was not going to cry, not in the doctor's office, not in the elevator, not anywhere. I would handle this, just like I'd handled everything else. I was Erin Foster, and I could deal with anything I had to. Even dying.

When I was sixteen, and daddy thought I had become too fond of my long blonde hair, he sat me down beside him on the porch. He looked at me for a long time.

"You're really a pretty girl, Erin."

I'd been told that I was pretty as long as I could remember. Geoff McCormack, the quarterback on our football team, told me that. I was homecoming queen. I knew that I was pretty.

"Let me tell you about pretty," he said. "It'll give you about a thirty-second head start. Sometime in those thirty seconds, you're going to have to prove that you're also smart. You don't, you'll be just another pretty girl."

Maybe I'd just imagined it, but I remember that then he looked toward the house where my mother was.

That may have been as important a conversation as I ever had with daddy. I thought about it and decided that I wanted more than to be Geoff's wife and live my life beside the country club swimming pool while he ran the Ford dealership. I didn't know what I wanted, but it had to be more than that. That was the first step that brought me to the city.

I got to the elevator without crying. The door opened as soon as I punched the button, and I stepped inside. I felt tears running down my cheeks. I wiped them off and waited for the elevator to get to the first floor. The doctor couldn't be sure. In fact, he was probably wrong. I felt fine. I had felt fine when my internist said that my checkup showed something that needed to be followed up on.

"It's probably nothing," she said. "I just like to be careful." And she sent me to Dr. Belzear. And he said it was probably nothing, but then he said that it was something, something that would kill me in six to nine months. I didn't believe him. I couldn't believe him.

I stepped out into the chilled March wind and walked back to the office. If there were tears, the wind dried them. It was only a few blocks to Argon Partners, the consulting firm I worked for. In those blocks, I didn't feel the wind or think about the cold. I was trying to think about my life.

I stopped outside the door to my building and took a breath. I wanted to make sure that everyone who saw me saw the Erin Foster that they knew. The one they called *Erinite* behind her back, all sharp-edged and hard. I had colleagues and associates at Argon Partners; I didn't have any close friends. It didn't bother me that they didn't want to be my friend. What I wanted was a partnership, and it looked like I was going to get one long before any of my peers.

Argon was always full of activity. Most people learned within days that if you weren't busy, you needed to look busy. As I went in, I wondered how many of the people striding purposefully down the hall were actually going somewhere and whether the file folders each of them carried has something to do with anything. I wanted to keep thinking that I could go on being busy, being successful, but I kept thinking about Dr. Belzear and six to nine months.

I picked up my phone messages and started to my office. Frank Jessep stopped me in the hall to tell me about the disaster Linc Thomas was making of the Amory Manufacturing engagement.

"The guy's a total screw-up," he said. "You think you can find some time to give him a hand before he blows the account."

I nodded, just as I always did. If something went wrong, I was the go-to person if it didn't require a partner. I liked it that way. I told Frank I'd get with Linc and see what was going on.

When I got to my desk, I sorted the messages. Two from clients. One from my mother. Almost all of my childhood, my mother had been a distant image, someone who was married to my father. Most of the time it was as if we were sitting on opposite sides of a wall; occasionally, daddy would carry messages between us. What little she had to say to me usually turned on my being a lady, sitting with my legs together, and finding the right husband. She had liked my being homecoming queen, but she had ignored the fact that I was valedictorian. For some reason, since daddy died, she had taken to calling me. The conversations were short, filled with silences, and usually left me feeling that less than nothing had really been said. Now, most of the time, I didn't answer the phone when she called or call her back.

In the next two hours I returned phone calls, read emails, and left a voice mail for Linc to see me tomorrow. I got a memo about an association meeting that needed a speaker next January. One of the partners wanted to know if I could do it. I started to reply. Then I stopped. January was nine months away. Could I really make an appointment for a time when I'm not supposed to be alive? All of the sadness of the day rose up in my chest, and I dissolved into wracking sobs.

The phone rang, and I just sat there, my head in my hands. Sobbing. This was the first day of the end of my life.

I had been taught a lot of things in my life, not counting all of the business and finance courses at the University. I had been taught by my mother how to act like a lady. How to sit. How to walk. I'd been taught to deal honestly with people by my daddy; so far as he was concerned anybody who didn't keep his word was just an oxygen thief. I'd been taught a gentle love by Geoff, one that fulfilled us but made no demands we couldn't handle. I had even been taught, by the examples of my grandmother and my grandfather, how to die with an unstrained dignity. But nobody had taught me how to live until I died.

After I left the office that day, I went home. My condo was a sign, one that all of my preparation had paid off, that I was no longer just a blonde MBA, but I had accomplished something. When I had gone home and told my parents that I was looking for a condo to buy, Mother said, "but what will you do with it when you get married?" All Daddy said was that I should make sure that I got one with good security.

That night I sat there, staring at the big buildings beyond my window, trying to make sense of what I had learned that day. A part of me said that I couldn't be dying. Not yet. I was only thirty-one. Another part of me kept hearing Dr. Belzear say that there was no doubt. It was cancer. It would kill me.

One of my problems is, I suppose, that I don't drink. In the books and movies, people faced with tragedy would drink themselves into a stupor, and in the stupor, they would quit thinking. When they woke up, and the racing thoughts surfaced through the pain of the hangover, they would do it again. I knew that was no solution, but I also knew I had no other solutions. I just sat and watched the big buildings, noticing that in the condos across the way the lights came on and went off. There were signs of life there, life that would last more than six or nine months.

The next morning, I pulled myself out of bed and got ready for work, just as I usually did. I ate breakfast and dressed. I put my makeup on carefully. It was the mask that would make today's Erin Foster look just like yesterday's Erin Foster, even though I knew I wasn't.

When I got to the office, Linc Thomas was sitting in the side chair at my desk. I looked at my watch. It was 8:30. He looked at his watch.

Linc was the male equivalent of the pretty girl who had always gotten by on being pretty. He dressed well. He knew how to order dinner in a good restaurant. He played an appropriate game of golf, good enough to provide some competition, but not so good as to beat the client. He was great at cocktail party small talk. The problem was that when it came to actually doing business, he acted as if he didn't have a brain in his head. Some of the people in the office called him "Scarecrow." I didn't call him anything. I tried not to think about him unless I was told to.

“Frank asked me to check into the Amory Manufacturing account for him. What’s happening?”

About six different expressions flashed across Linc’s face. The last one was anger.

“If Frank wants to know about Amory Manufacturing, why doesn’t he ask me?”

“Don’t know. He just asked me to do it. What’s happening?”

For a minute I thought Linc was going to get up and leave. Then he evidently thought better of it. One thing worse than having to discuss Amory with me was being sent back by Frank to discuss it with me.

“Everything’s cool on Amory. We might have to slip a couple of our milestones, but we can make it up.”

“What does Amory management think of that?” I asked, trying to keep a neutral tone. Everything was not cool if we were behind schedule on the project.

“I’m setting up a meeting next week to discuss it with them. It’s not a big deal.”

“Okay. Maybe not. Could you send me your last couple of status reports and whatever you’re proposing as the new schedule?”

Technically, Linc and I were on the same level. We were both consultants and not partners. But I had said the magic words: “Frank asked me...” There was no way he could refuse, but he certainly didn’t want to be seen as taking orders from me. He looked down.

“Yeah. Sure.”

“Could you do it this morning? I need to get back to Frank.”

His head snapped back up, a red flush creeping into his face.

“I’ll get it to you when I can,” he said. Then he stood up and left the office.

For a few minutes, I felt good. I was doing my job. I was just like I was before seeing Dr. Belzear. But the feeling didn’t last.

"It's no big deal," he'd said. He didn't know just how small a deal it was to me right then.

I sent an email to Frank, telling him that I'd met with Linc and that the Amory project was going to miss one or more milestones. I told him I'd check Linc's revised schedule and let him know what was happening. I wondered if I should call Mother. The first she heard about my cancer shouldn't be somebody calling to say that I was dead, but I didn't know how I'd get through a conversation with her. I tried to work on my own projects.

After two hours of fumbling from one file to another, I knew that my mind could not focus on anybody's problems but my own. That there were millions of dollars at stake made no difference, and certainly, the fact that success in helping a client make or save those millions would move me closer to a partnership didn't make a difference; I wouldn't be alive to claim it.

I called Frank Jessup to see if he had a minute for me. He did.

Frank was living proof that Daddy was right. He was one of the three partners who interviewed me just before I graduated from college, and in that first interview, it was obvious that he was perfectly happy judging the book by its cover. He seemed surprised that the female partner in the group warmed to me, and in the end, the three partners agreed that I should be offered a position. It was one of four offers I received, and while it didn't have the highest starting salary, it offered the broadest experience. Argon helped high-profile clients with serious problems or amazing opportunities. Every engagement was the Mount Everest of its type.

But it didn't take Frank long to accept that I wasn't "just another pretty girl." I still caught him looking at me occasionally, but that didn't bother me. So far as I knew, Frank was absolutely faithful to his wife and four children.

Now he was staring at his hands folded together on his desk.

"I don't know. I was going to just keep working as long as I could. You know, live until I die."

He shook his head. “There’s no way you can make this funny. Don’t try.”

I started to tell him that trying to crack a joke was my way of not breaking down completely. Instead, I just nodded.

“I don’t think I’ll be doing a lot of good here. My mind won’t turn loose the fact that I have just this little time left and that there’s something I should be doing with it. I don’t know what I’m going to do, but I don’t think it’ll be here.”

He nodded.

“You know you’re welcome to stay as long as you can. Or you can take some time off and then come back when you have it figured out.”

“Thank you. I appreciate that.”

“Do you have enough to live on?”

I hadn’t thought about it. Even when you’re dying, you have to pay to live. I had several thousand dollars in savings and some stocks, mostly in companies I had done work for. That, the car and the furniture was all I really owned. There wasn’t a lot of equity in the condo.

“I think so. I don’t know,” I said.

He nodded. Frank was a problem solver. He had been the youngest partner in Argon’s history, and—aside from the two founding partners who still worked when they liked—he was the most powerful person in the company.

“With everything you’ve done for Argon, you shouldn’t have to worry about money.”

I thanked him and started to get up. Then I noticed that there were tears in his eyes.

“I thought you would be properly rewarded. You would be a partner.” He shook his head. “I’ll have you a check by the end of the day.”

He looked back down at his hands on the desk. I couldn’t see his face.

I spent the rest of the day trying to decide what to do. I couldn't stay at Argon with people watching me die. I didn't think I could hole up in the condo until they had to take me somewhere. I couldn't go back to Smithfield and live with Mother. But, with all the things I knew I couldn't do, I couldn't think of one thing I should do. Before I thought of something, it was the end of the day, and the support staff was leaving. Most of the consultants would be there for a while, some late into the night. That was how you earned your stripes at Argon.

As I was putting my personal things into a box, Frank stepped into my office.

"Do you know what you're going to do?"

I shook my head. "I know I can't hang around here. The word will get out. I don't want a bunch of people pitying me."

"I figured." He sat down in the chair beside my desk. "I had an idea that might help for a little while."

He put an envelope on the desk.

"There's a check in there. It should help. Also, there're directions to a cabin we have in the mountains. And the key to the door. It's the quietest, most peaceful place I know. I thought you might want to spend a week or two—or as long as you like—up there."

Frank didn't wait for my answer. He got up and left. I sat there, feeling as if I had just lost my last connection to the real world.

I was nine when my grandmother—Daddy's mother—died. She had been dying for a while; her last months were spent propped up in bed. She usually had a stack of books along with bottles of pills on the table beside her bed. Propped on those pillows, she seemed a lot smaller than she was before she got sick, but she still smiled, and when I stopped in to see her after school, she always wanted to know what I had learned that day. She never asked me if I had had a good day.

"You never really know what a good day is," she told me one day as I was sitting on the edge of her bed. "Some of the days I liked the least turned out to be very important. Like the first time I actually failed an English test. My mother grounded me for two weeks, and I hated English. I hated English tests. And I really didn't like my mother very much. But I learned that you tend to get out of things what you put into them. If I studied like I was supposed to, I wouldn't fail tests. Works out that way all through life. Turned out that was a good day for me."

We would talk about her life and what she had done, about my life and what I would do, and every day, when I was about to leave, she would give me a hug, pulling me close to her and enveloping me in the lilac smell that was always in the room. She would hold me for a minute, and before she let me go, she would whisper in my ear: "Live a good life, my darling."

She had done that up until the day before she died. I went to school the next morning, and Daddy came to get me before school was out.

"Mama died a little while ago," he said. "I thought you might want to come on home."

We went to Grandmother's, and I stayed up in her room while the neighbors came and went, bringing plates of food, whispering their condolences to Daddy and Granddaddy, and leaving with lists of things that needed to be done. I cried for a while. I could still smell the lilac, but I knew it wouldn't be long before the lilac would also be gone.

I lay on her bed. Thinking of my grandma and hearing her tell me to live a good life.

The funeral was two days later. We all dressed up and got in the Cadillac that the funeral director sent. It seemed like most of the town was at the church; a lot of the people were wiping their eyes. It was the first time I had been to a funeral. It was my first experience with death. I didn't like either one of them.

It took me a long time to understand that Grandma had known she was dying, but she decided to make the effort to keep living, really living, as long as she could. Daddy told me that the doctor, when he told her she was so sick, had said that she had about a year to live. For most of that year, she still played bridge with her friends, just as she had for most of her life. She went out to lunch, even when they had to push her in a wheelchair the last few times, and she was always more interested in the people around her than she was herself.

If you asked how she was, she said, "Fine."

I sat in my condo that night staring at the big buildings out the window, thinking about Grandma. Then about Granddaddy. He did what he usually did as long as he could—pulled the weeds from the grass, walked downtown to the grocery or barbershop, visited Grandmother's grave. Finally, he couldn't do any of those things. He could just sit in his chair. But if you asked him how he was, he said, "Fine."

I didn't know how Grandma or Granddaddy could say fine, knowing that they weren't "fine." They were dying.

Somewhere in my desk, I had a schedule. It was life mapped out by year. What I wanted to accomplish. Where I wanted to be. Some time, several years ago, I had felt confident enough to map out my future. That was when I thought I had a future.

I decided to accept Frank's offer and go to his mountain cabin. It was, he said, a peaceful place. I desperately wanted some peace.

I only took a few things to the cabin. Some jeans and sweaters. A jacket. A few books. At the last minute, I picked up my Bible, the one I'd taken with me to Sunday School every Sunday when I was growing up. I hadn't opened it often then; I hadn't opened it at all since I had come to the city. But I was trying to adapt myself to some vision of what people did when they were dying. I thought reading the Bible was something they did.

I noticed when I unpacked that I was already changing. I was the one who packed at least one large suitcase or maybe two when I went home from school for the weekend. I worried about being dressed properly for whatever occasion. Now I wasn't. And I didn't expect many occasions at the cabin.

I had also brought a bottle of sleeping pills. My doctor had prescribed them when I was having insomnia, and I'd never thrown them out. I thought I might need to take one sometime. Now I wondered if I didn't need them all.

I hadn't known what to expect as I drove to the cabin. I had seen "cottages" at the shore that were really very large houses. But Frank's cabin was what he said it was. A very small house, stuck at the end of a path, a long way from anything or anybody. It was, I suppose, peaceful. I would have said "isolated."

It only took me a few minutes to move in, to bring in my clothes and a couple of bags of food. I had no idea how long I would be at the cabin. I had no idea where I would go when I left.

I tried to read my Bible, but I didn't know where to start. Wherever I turned, it seemed that they were talking about somebody else. Finally, I shut the Bible and sat in the chair by the window, staring through the old glass that bent my view of everything in the yard. The yard was bare, with a sprinkling of brown weeds and a few scrub trees. Spring had not really arrived in the mountains, so there was no life to relieve the remains of everything that had died last year.

I knew that the woods beyond the drive stretched for several miles before abruptly stopping at the nearest paved road. Once that two-lane path I'd driven down had been the way in and the way out for the family that worked the little farm. Now, for the most part, it was neither, and the fields behind the house were overgrown.

I tried to focus on what I would do, to think of something in the future, but the sun shining through the grimy glass made me feel warm and relaxed, and my mind floated from place to place and from time to time. Occasionally I would think of something I regretted, when I should have done something differently, but it was easy to dismiss those now. There wasn't time to do anything differently.

I sat at the window for several hours, more relaxed than I had been since Dr. Belzear delivered my death sentence. It occurred to me that I had not seen a bird or an animal while I sat at the window. There was nothing to remind me that some things would live while I died.

I warmed a can of soup for supper, then tried to read for a while, but I couldn't concentrate. I wondered if the next six months were going to be like this, and if they were, would it be better just to take the pills and not have to deal with every passing day.

The next morning, I fixed coffee and returned to my spot at the window, staring at the yard. It was, as it had been the day before, very still, just something to stare at to keep from staring at nothing. Then I thought I saw something. It may have been a deer or—more likely—a gust of wind in the trees. But something had moved.

I went to the door of the cabin and looked at the edge of the woods where the movement had been. I edged out onto the uneven, plank porch. It only took a minute to make out a patch of print fabric between the branches of a scrub tree, then a bit of a face.

"Hello," I said. "Who's there?"

Nobody responded.

I took another step forward.

"Look, I know you're out there. Show yourself."

The branches rustled, and a girl stepped out. She was maybe eleven or twelve. The shift that she was wearing hung straight down on her thin frame, and she was barefoot despite the cold morning and the colder night. Her pencil-thin arms were bare.

"Who are you?" I asked. "What are you doing here?"

The little girl edged out of the woods, and I stepped off the porch and walked to her. She stopped, as if she were about to run. I stopped; then I turned back to the house.

"Come on in," I said. "It's warmer inside." I didn't turn around until I was on the porch about to open the door. When I did, I saw that she was coming toward the house, very slowly. As I waited for her, I saw that she looked like a collection of badly fitted parts. Her eyes, large and dark, seemed too big for her face. Her cheeks were hollow, and her arms and legs seemed to be no more than skin-covered bone. Her dress was homemade, just some material sewn together with holes for the head and arms. She had purple bruises on her arms and a fading purple splotch next to her mouth. Whoever this child was, she had been treated badly.

I held the door open for her to go into the house, then I went to the cabinet and got a cup.

"You drink coffee? It'll warm you up."

She nodded, standing in the middle of the room, perfectly still. I brought a cup of coffee to her and gently pushed her toward a chair. She sat down, wrapping her hands around the cup of steaming coffee and holding it close to her. I sat down and waited for her to drink some of the coffee.

"What's your name?" I asked.

For a moment, she just stared into the coffee cup.

"Doris. My name is Doris."

I just nodded and sat there. I'd learned long ago that sometimes the best way to get information is to wait. Some people can't stand silence, so they talk a lot.

Doris looked around. "Do you live here?"

"No. I'm just staying here for a while."

Doris just nodded and sipped her coffee.

I got up and walked to the window, looking for other movements. I knew there had to be reason that Doris had spent the night in the woods.

"What were you doing in the woods?"

"I ran away."

It was a very quiet, matter-of-fact statement, but I'd never known anybody who had had to run away. At least until I had left everything and everybody I knew to come to this cabin.

"What were you running away from?"

It seemed like the question that had to be asked, but even as I asked it, I wasn't sure I wanted to hear the answer. I had enough to deal with.

The thin, little girl turned away. Her shoulders began to shake, and I could hear her sobs.

"I have to leave. He'll find me here," she said. Her breaths were coming in gasps between the sobs.

I walked over and knelt beside her.

"Who'll find you, Doris?"

She sat straight up, trying to stop the crying. She wiped her eyes with the back of her hand.

"Al," she said. "He was staying with my mama, but my mama died."

I touched the bruises on her arm.

"Did Al do this to you?"

Doris nodded.

"He says now that Mama's gone, I have to be his woman, and I have to do what he wants. If I don't, he hits me."

"When did your mother die?"

"Back before Christmas. He hit Mama, too, but he didn't try to get on top of me until after Mama was gone."

"How old are you, Doris."

"I'm thirteen. Al says I'm a woman now."

I just nodded. I didn't know what to say. When I was thirteen, I was in the Girl Scouts and on the Youth League Soccer team. I'd probably had some thoughts about being a woman, but I couldn't remember any. I walked back to the window and stood there, staring out.

"Why are you looking out the window?" Doris asked. "Are you looking for Al?"

"No. I'm just looking out the window and thinking. It seems like what I ought to do right now."

I heard Doris put her cup in the sink; then, she was standing beside me at the window.

"I don't see anything," she said.

"I don't either."

To Doris, the emptiness on the other side of the window meant that for that moment she didn't have to be afraid. For me, it was simply emptiness. I knew that I couldn't let her go back into the woods, especially with the cold night coming, but it took me a while to convince her that nobody lived in the cabin most of the time, so this was probably not the place he'd look for her.

Finally, she relaxed, and I showed her the tiny bathroom and gave her some of my clothes. I knew that they would swallow her, but they were warmer than what she had. After she was bathed and shown the other bedroom, I went back to the sofa, caught in a strange feeling.

I'd never been indecisive. I was taught by Daddy to look at the facts, make a decision, and go on. If I found I'd made the wrong decision, to make another one. That had worked well for me at Argon. I was known for being decisive, perhaps even ruthless. Look at the facts, and do what it takes. The problem was that I had too few facts and no precedents. There was nothing about Doris that I could relate to, except—maybe—for the fact that she was afraid.

The more that I had told myself that I wasn't afraid, the more I insisted to myself that I could handle what I'd been told, the more I knew I was lying. At least Doris wasn't trying to deceive herself. She was afraid, and she had admitted it. However, the fact that she was afraid had caused her to take some sort of action: she ran away.

I began thinking about what I did know, the facts. Doris was with me. She was probably being chased by a pedophile named Al. I had no experience in dealing with a child at any age. There was no phone in the cabin and no cell phone signal, so calling the authorities was out of the question, as was simply sending her on her way tomorrow. Finally, I decided that the only rational thing to do was to take Doris into town and let her tell her story to the authorities. They could take it from there, and I could come back to the cabin and decide what I was going to do.

I went to the bedroom and saw Doris lying in bed. Her eyes were still open. I told her that when she woke up, we would go into town and find her a safe place. She just said, "Thank you, ma'am." I went back to the window, hoping that the tiredness I was feeling would let me get some sleep. At some point, I dozed off, sitting in the chair by the window.

I don't know how much later it was, maybe two hours, when I woke up again. My neck was stiff from sleeping in the chair. I heard a noise coming from the other bedroom, a fretful moaning.

While I was asleep, it had gotten colder, and the wooden floors were icy to my bare feet. I peeked into the bedroom. Doris was asleep, but not comfortably. She had thrashed around in the bed until the covers were in a tangle around her. The noise she was making was between a whimper and a moan. I leaned over to straighten the covers, and as my hand brushed her face, I felt a feverish heat. She had a temperature, probably from her exposure to the cold. I finished straightening the covers and went into the kitchen to find some aspirin.

I remembered that when I was a little girl, my mother gave me aspirin to bring down the fever. It seemed like when I was in bed with a fever, my mother could accept me, or maybe it was just that she could understand me. She brought aspirin and orange juice and washed my face with a cool cloth. Sometimes she would hold me to her, humming a church song. Then I would get well, and we would each sit on our sides of the wall.

I found the aspirin, got a glass of water, and went back to Doris. I roused her enough to get the aspirin and a swallow of water in her, then sat there as she went back to sleep. Then I went to bed, but I couldn't sleep.

A few hours later, before the sun was up, I got up and went to check on Doris. It seemed that the fever had broken. The girl's hair, washed and clean when she went to bed, was matted around her face with sweat. She had thrown most of the covers off. But she was sleeping peacefully.

I made me some coffee, trying to figure out what I was going to do. Doris probably wasn't going to be in any shape to make the trip into town, and even if she felt better when she got up, the fever could come back in the afternoon. But I wondered if she would be better off in town if she needed to see the doctor.

I tried to think about this as I had been taught to think. I was a consultant; my job was to define and solve problems. The problem was that there was a sick, mistreated child in the bedroom that needed a safe place and someone to take care of her.

But another part of me was whispering that that was her problem. My problem was that I was dying, and Doris was a distraction. I needed to decide what I was going to do with the rest of my life, or if I really wanted to live whatever the rest of my life might be. I sat by the window with my coffee, watching the shafts of light coming through the trees.

I thought about Mother. Why had she changed so much after Daddy died? Why now, instead of all those years when I was growing up, was she trying to talk to me. We'd spent nearly thirty years building that wall. I wasn't sure that it would ever come down. And now, having refused to talk with her for months, what would I say if I did call her? "Hi, how are you. I'm dying from cancer. Thought you should know." Sooner or later, I would have to call her. Or if I didn't, someone else would.

I heard a stirring behind me. Doris was standing in the door, paler even than she was the day before. I pulled a throw off the back of the sofa and wrapped it around her.

"Would you like some breakfast? I have some cereal here. I'm not much for breakfast."

Doris nodded and went to the table. I poured the cereal and milk, and then I went back to the window. Occasionally I would turn and look at Doris. Draped in the blanket, she looked even smaller, the big eyes taking up most of her face. She looked down into the bowl, slowly lifting the spoon to her mouth, making certain that none of the milk or cereal spilled over. It was as if she were trying to contract herself into an even smaller space.

I wondered if this child would ever have a normal childhood, or if the only thing left for her was being assaulted by her stepfather until he killed her, or—having stood all she could—she killed him. It was death one way or another. Maybe this child was pulling herself into a smaller and smaller space until, if she could, she would make herself not exist at all.

The space we occupy means something. I had been a daughter and had people who loved me. I had been a friend—even a girlfriend. I had been successful. I had been happy. This child had none of this. I was going to die, but that had always been true. It was just long before I had expected it. But looking at Doris, I began to think that I should be thankful that I had had an opportunity to live.

I walked over to the table and put my hand against her face. She was cool. She leaned just a little into my hand. I pulled my hand away and walked back to the window. I'd never been tempted to pick up strays when I was a child; I didn't need or want a pet. I felt the same way about Doris. My obligation was to get her somewhere safe. Then I would have done all that anybody could expect me to do. Nobody could expect me to take on another responsibility when I was trying to figure out how I was going to die. I slumped against the window frame, wondering just how many days of this I'd have to put up with and hoping it wasn't a lot.

I pressed my head into the rough window frame, trying to use the sensation from outside of me to overwhelm the feelings inside me. The little girl sitting at the table was not a stray, some feral dog or cat. She was a child whose childhood was being wiped out. I pushed harder against the window frame, wishing that I could decide which of us I was going to worry about.

First, it was the vibration of the window frame. Then I heard the sound. I looked out the window and saw an old truck coming down the path, a dirty black with one fender gray. It bounced from one side of the path to the other.

I turned around. Doris had heard it, too.

"Doris, come here." I pointed out the window. "Is that Al?"

I already knew it was. There was no reason for anyone to come to the cabin, especially in a hurry.

By the time Doris had gotten to the window, the truck had stopped in the yard, and a man stumbled out. He was gaunt, sickly thin, dressed in dirty overalls and an undershirt. There was a stubble of beard on his face.

"Doris," he yelled. "Doris, I know you in there. You come out right now."

Doris moved closer to me, trying to fold tightly enough that she would be out of sight. I already knew that the cabin didn't have a back door. I looked at the back wall again, trying to will some sort of exit away from the man coming toward the cabin.

There wasn't one, just a wall of rough wood and window too small to crawl out of.

"Go into the bedroom, Doris. Don't come out, no matter what." She went to the bedroom. I went back to the window. Yesterday I had been wondering whether it was worth trying to live another year or another month. Now, all I could think about was how I was going to keep Doris—and me—alive. Suddenly I felt like I had something more to lose.

The man walked toward the porch. "If you don't come out right now, Doris, I'm going to come in and get you. You got no right to run off from me."

He was only about 10 feet from the steps.

I grabbed a kitchen knife from the counter and went to the door. I held the knife behind me as I stepped out on the porch.

"What do you want?" I said. As scared as I felt, at least my voice didn't shake.

"You got my woman in there, don't you?"

"Look, mister, I don't know what you want, but you're on private property. If you don't get off right now, I'm going to call the sheriff."

He looked around the house.

"I don't see any wires for a telephone. I know you got Doris here. A man up the road saw her coming this way. She couldn't have gone a whole lot further."

He started to step toward the porch. He was close enough that I could see the brown streak of tobacco stain running from the corner of his mouth down his chin.

"Don't come any closer."

Al just stared at me.

"I don't know who you are, Ma'am, and I don't want no trouble with you, but I'm going to take Doris back home. It's my right."

He took another step toward the porch. I stepped back into the door frame, preparing to close the door.

"Don't come any closer," I said. "Just get in that wreck you came in and leave."

He took two quick steps and jumped up on the porch, his hand out to grab me. I stepped back inside the cabin, and just as he reached in, I threw my body against the heavy wooden door. It slammed, and I heard the crunch of bone as it hit his wrist. He screamed, and his hand was caught in the door. I put all of my weight against the door, grinding it into his wrist. Then I lifted the knife and drove it into his hand. He screamed louder. The blood seeped around the edge of the knife blade. A small part of my brain registered that the trickle of blood meant that I hadn't hit an artery. I kept my weight against the door, listening to the curses and the screams.

I pulled the knife out, none too gently; then, I pressed the point against his hand, as close to the wrist as I could get.

"I can cut your hand off," I said. "Or would you rather just go away." I pressed the point of the knife a little deeper into his skin.

He didn't answer. The screaming and cursing had gotten quieter. I thought that he had gone into shock. I pulled the door open, holding the knife in front of me. Al had been leaning against the door frame; now, he slid to the floor, pulling his broken wrist close to him.

I stepped forward, putting the point of the knife to his neck and pressing just enough for the point to make a dent in the skin.

"You deserve to die," I said. "But I don't want to be the one to kill you, and that little girl in there doesn't need to have to think of you again, dead or alive."

He just looked at me. There was no bravado left. His eyes were wide with fear. Sweat was pouring down his face, and blood from the wound in his hand seeped around his fingers.

“So here’s your choice. You can get up and go back to whatever hell hole you came from and leave Doris alone, or I’ll cut your throat right now.”

He looked up, his eyes wide with pain.

“She’s here, ain’t she?”

“Yes, she is, but she won’t be for long. I’ll give you ten minutes to get out of here. Then I’m going to stop by the sheriff’s office in town and give him a statement. I’m sure he’ll be looking for you soon, so you probably should start running and just keep going.”

I pressed the knife a little harder until a drop of blood ran down his neck. I stared into his eyes for a minute, just to make sure that the fear was still there. Then I went back inside, slamming the door. I heard him drag himself off the porch, and then the truck started up. Al was leaving.

Doris ran over to me and buried her face in my robe. She was sobbing. I pulled the little girl to me, holding her close and stroking her hair. We slowly rocked back and forth.

“You’re going to be all right, Doris. We’re going to get my things together and go into town. We’ll make sure you’re safe. And I have to make a phone call.”

We walked over to the window and watched the truck creeping up the path.

DORIS

The preacher looked too young to know much about dying, but he kept talking about it. Behind the big pulpit at the Smithfield Methodist Church, he looked like a boy playing at being a preacher. From where I was sitting on the front row, I could hardly see his head. Miss Ava said that he hadn't been at the church long and almost didn't know Miss Erin.

After talking about death and hope for a while, he started talking about what a nice person Miss Erin was, how she'd spent her last days giving to somebody else, and when he said that, I think everybody in the church looked at me. There were a lot of people there, some of them Miss Erin's age and some of them Miss Ava's age. There were some my age, like my friend Michelle, but not many. I guess being dead is something fourteen-year-olds don't want to think about unless they have to.

Before the funeral started, before they closed the casket, I went up to the front of the church and looked one more time at Miss Erin. I just stood there looking, while some other people came up. They just walked around me. One lady patted me on the arm and told me how pretty Miss Erin look. She did. In that casket, she was as pretty as she was when I first saw her, maybe prettier because she didn't have on any makeup then. And now there was a little smile on her face like she had seen something good. I prayed that she had. I prayed that Heaven was everything that Miss Ava and Miss Erin said it was.

It seemed like a long time before the preacher quit talking, and some men in dark blue suits rolled the casket out of the church. Another man in a blue suit stood at the end of the pew and motioned for us to come. It seemed like every eye in the church was staring at me, maybe wondering why I got to walk out first with Miss Ava. I tried to hold my head up, just like Miss Ava did and like Miss Erin would've wanted me to. When we got to the door, I could hear the other people getting ready to come out behind us. We all got into cars and went to the cemetery and sat down on wooden folding chairs under a little tent. Most of the people at the church hadn't come to the cemetery.

I just looked at the wooden casket sitting on the straps over the grave. I didn't want to believe that Miss Erin was in it, but I knew she was. The little-boy preacher started talking again, about what a pretty and nice person she was. What he said was right, but it wasn't near enough. I thought of a hundred things that I wanted him to say.

I felt the tears sliding down my face, and Miss Ava reached over and took my hand. She was crying, too. In fact, I couldn't think of anything that would be right to do except cry. I'd lost Miss Erin, and I hadn't known her near long enough. Miss Ava had lost her daughter, and she'd told me she didn't know her near well enough. She also told me that death didn't wait around for us to do the things we ought to.

The preacher finally said a prayer, and the gray-haired man standing at the end of the grave nodded to some other men in blue suits, and they started lowering the casket into the grave. Lord, it was slow. It seemed like forever before Miss Ava and I stood up and walked to the edge of the grave. We didn't throw any dirt or flowers in; we just stood at the edge and said goodbye one more time.

The people who had come to the cemetery gathered around us, the older women smelling like sweet flowers. Some of them bent down and hugged me. They talked to Miss Ava for a while; then we walked back to the big black car that was waiting for us.

On the way back to Miss Ava's house, she put her arm around me and pulled me close to her. We cried all the way.

The first time I saw the house in Smithfield, I almost couldn't believe it. I'd never seen a house that big or that white. When Miss Erin and I got there, Miss Ava was out in the front yard waiting for us. She'd known we were coming, except she didn't know me from a bunch of turnips. I was just somebody Miss Erin said she was bringing with her.

It was about a week after she'd chased Al off from that little cabin before we were able to leave. First, the people Miss Erin went to in town said I had to go to a foster home. Then there were some things that they had to do in court, but finally, the judge shook his head and said, "This little girl has been through enough," and he told Miss Erin that if she would leave an address and phone number with him, he'd work it out with the county people.

Then we left.

I didn't know if I'd been through enough or not. I'd never known any kind of life except for the one I'd had with my mama, then when my mama died, with Al. When it was just mama and me, I'd liked it. Sometimes mama worried about getting us enough to eat when the little garden didn't have anything in it. But she took care of me. I didn't like it when it was just Al and me. I don't know where I was going when I ran away that day, but I knew I couldn't stay around Al.

When I was little, mama read me books, and in the books, the people or animals or fish were usually happy. Then I went to school, and I saw that almost everybody there wore clean clothes, so I tried to make sure my dress was clean every day. And I tried to make sure I knew my lessons every day.

When mama died, Al made me stay at home, but when he went out, I still read my books, and sometimes I would work on my arithmetic. I wanted to go back to school, and I didn't want to be behind when I did.

I asked mama one time why she'd married Al. He was mean to her; sometimes he hit her. All she said was that we were women, and sometimes women needed somebody to take care of them. That didn't seem right to me. I'd rather not have somebody taking care of me if it meant they could hit me or push me on the bed and get on top of me.

Sometimes in the night, I heard Mama begging Al to stop. I don't know what he was doing, but Mama was crying. I wanted to run in there and help her, but I didn't.

Miss Erin told me we were going to see her mama, that we'd stay there, at least for a while. So we left that little cabin and drove for a long time before we got to Smithfield. I thought about what Miss Erin's mama would look like. I knew she'd be old because Miss Erin was about as old as my mama, but I was surprised when I met her.

My mama wasn't old, but she looked old. She'd had a hard life, and it showed on her. Her face was thin. Her body was thin. And I don't remember her smiling much in those last years.

Miss Ava was old, but she didn't look old. When I saw her standing in the front yard, I couldn't believe that she was Miss Erin's mama. Her hair was brown with a little gray in it, and she was wearing pants and a white shirt. She looked like she was getting ready to go somewhere.

When we stopped in front of the house, Miss Erin patted me on the arm and told me to wait at the car for a minute. Then she got out and went up to her mother. I couldn't see Miss Erin's face, but her mama had a big smile on hers, and she held her arms open. Miss Erin threw her arms around her mother, and they hugged. They hugged for a long time, then Miss Erin turned her mama loose and motioned for me to get out. When I got to them, both of them were crying. But they were both smiling, too, so I figured that it was alright that I was there.

"Doris, meet my mother," Miss Erin said. Then she leaned close to me and whispered, "You're going to like her a lot."

That first night at Miss Ava's house, I laid real quiet in my bed. I told myself that if I didn't move or make any noise, if I didn't make any bother for anybody, they might let me stay with them. I laid there without moving even my fingers, just like I used to. When I lived with Al after mama died, I'd lay as quiet as I could so he wouldn't bother me. Sometimes he didn't. It was the best thing I could think to do.

I just laid there, still, feeling the cool sheets and the soft bed beneath me. I didn't ever want to leave.

Miss Erin had told me she was sick, that the doctor said she didn't have a long time to live, but when she told me, she didn't seem that sad. She said it like it was just a fact, like whether it was raining or not. She said she wanted to make sure she used what time she had left to do what she needed to do.

Every night when I went to bed, Miss Erin would come up to my room, and we'd read the Bible. Sometimes she'd read it to me; sometimes, she'd stretch out across the bed and listen to me read it to her. One night I was reading to her about the parable of the talents, and when I finished, she nodded and said, "That's about the way it is."

I looked at her. I didn't know what she meant.

"It's just that some people are given a lot, and God expects them to do a lot with it. And some people are just given a little, but God still expects them to do something. I always thought I was given a lot, but then, when the doctor told me I was sick, I thought I wasn't given much at all. That's when I went up to that cabin, because I didn't figure there was anything I could do. I guess I was going to just sit up there until I died."

"Like the servant who buried his talent?"

She nodded. "Just like that. And then you showed up. I knew there was something I could do with the time I had left. You know, you may have saved the rest of my life."

She pulled the covers up on me and gave me a kiss on the forehead. Nobody but Mama put me to bed or kissed me good-night until Miss Erin. In fact, it'd been a long time since I'd gone to bed without being scared. Now I just went off to sleep.

It was April when we got to Smithfield, too late for me to go to school. Since I hadn't been in school for about a year, Miss Erin and Miss Ava just decided to teach me at home. Miss Ava brought a school-teacher friend of hers in to give me some tests and find out what I knew. Then the teacher brought some books over, and I started studying every day. The school teacher said that I should go into the seventh grade when school started.

It was different in Smithfield than it was in the mountains. For one thing, it was hotter. And the farms around town were a lot bigger than the little plots we had in the mountains. But the biggest difference was how they talked—softer and slower than I was used to. In the mountains, it seemed like all the words had hard edges on them; in Smithfield, none of them did.

One day Miss Erin said we were going to the movies, and somebody named Carol Ann was going with us. I asked her who Carol Ann was, and she said she was a girl who lived in the neighborhood. Miss Erin said she thought it was time I made some friends so I'd know somebody when I went to school in September.

Turns out that Carol Ann was a girl about my age. She was bigger than me, and she had long blond hair that she kept playing with. I guess she was pretty, but it looked like she was about to say, "Don't mess with me," or something like that. Her mother brought her to Miss Erin's house and sort of pushed her through the door. She stood there, not saying anything until Miss Erin said, "Doris, this is Carol Ann. Carol Ann, this is Doris."

She still didn't say anything. Neither did I. I didn't know what to say. Miss Erin looked at each of us and shrugged.

"It's time to go to the movie," she said, putting an arm around each of us.

We went to the movie, and Miss Erin bought us each a popcorn and a drink. She made us sit beside each other, but Carol Ann still didn't have anything to say. When the movie was over, we walked Carol Ann to her house, then walked home.

"Did you like Carol Ann?" Miss Erin asked me.

"I guess. We didn't talk much."

Miss Erin stopped and looked at me.

"You're going to need to make some friends, Doris. Or at least one really good friend. I didn't think much about that when I was in school. Or even when I went to work. Now I wish I had."

I just nodded, and we walked on home.

About a week later, I saw Carol Ann and two other girls walking down the sidewalk. They were going to come right by Miss Ava's house, so I walked down to the end of the driveway. I wanted to do what Miss Erin said and try to make friends.

When they got almost to me, I said hello to Carol Ann.

She just looked at me like she couldn't quite make out who or what I was.

"Who's that?" one of the other girls said.

"Just somebody Erin brought home," Carol Ann said and kept walking.

I watched them walk down the sidewalk, giggling. One of the girls looked back over her shoulder at me. Then they giggled some more. I figured that Carol Ann probably wasn't going to be the real good friend Miss Erin was talking about.

But there was one girl in the neighborhood that I started talking to. Her daddy was the preacher at the Baptist church, and she was the same age I was.

I met her one day when I was walking around the neighborhood, just looking at all the big houses and wondering who lived in them. Just having houses side by side was something new for me. In the mountains, we couldn't even see our neighbors' houses, and Al didn't talk to them unless it was to argue about something. But in Smithfield, the houses were all lined up in a row back from the street behind the green grass yards with trees and flowers in front of the house. I thought they were beautiful.

As I passed one house, I saw a girl sitting in a swing with a big pad in front of her, drawing. I stopped for a minute. She looked up and waved at me. I waved back.

"Want to see what I'm drawing?" she asked.

I'd never been into any of the yards. I didn't know if I was allowed, but the girl seemed to want me to look at her picture, so I went up there. As I got closer, I saw that there was a wheelchair at the end of the swing. And I saw her legs dangling down from the swing like they weren't really attached to her body, like maybe somebody had pinned them their dress. But her face looked alive with a big smile. And she had a lot of long curly brown hair.

"My name's Michelle. What's yours?"

"Doris."

She nodded. "You live over at Miss Ava's, don't you?"

"Yes. I live with Miss Ava and Miss Erin." I waited to see what she was going to say next. I lived with Miss Ava and Miss Erin, but I wasn't sure I belonged there. I didn't know where I belonged since I was only there if they wanted me there. There wasn't anybody who had to put up with me.

Michelle turned her pad around so I could see it. She was drawing the birdbath that was sitting in front of the shrubs. It was funny how she could make what she drew in pencil look like concrete. All of the lines were there, and the shadow fell beside it. It looked just like the birdbath, except that she had put a bird in it, and there wasn't one.

"That's nice," I said. "You can really draw."

"I draw a lot. In the summer, I have a lot of time and not much to do, so mostly I draw."

"Did the bird fly away?"

"Not really. I just thought there ought to be a bird in the birdbath, so I put one in it. Nothing says I can't make something prettier than it really is."

We sat in the swing while Michelle finished her picture. I watched her make quick strokes with her pencil that somehow turned out to look like something. Finally, she put the pencils back in the box and closed the pad.

"You want to take a walk?" she asked. She looked over toward the wheelchair. "Or you can take a walk. I'll take a roll."

I didn't know what to say. I'd never talked to somebody who couldn't walk before, but Michelle didn't wait for me to say anything. She pulled the wheelchair around to the front of the swing, put her hands on the arms of the chair, and slid herself into it. She yelled to her mama that we were going to take a walk, and we headed down the sidewalk. I had to speed up a little just to stay up with her.

"I heard Daddy telling Mama that you lived in the mountains," she said.

I told her about living on a little farm in the mountains and how Smithfield was so different from that.

"Do you like the mountains better than here?"

"I don't think so. Sometimes the mountains are really pretty, I guess, but so's Smithfield. We don't have houses and yards in the mountains like you do here. It's all hills and rocks with a little patch of corn and beans wherever we can plant them."

Down the street, I saw Carol Ann and some of her friends, but they didn't pay any attention to us. They just kept walking.

We went all the way around the block with Michelle telling me who lived in each of the houses and something about them. One house had a lady who used to teach English in school, but she got sick and couldn't teach anymore. Now she had children come to her house in the summer and give book reports. If they did good, she'd give them something. Michelle said that she went there about every week and that I could go too if I wanted to.

Another house was where the owner of the town's biggest store lived. Michelle said he was really rich, and his wife was a drunk. He was always out around town, but nobody ever saw the wife anymore.

When we got back to her house, she asked me if I wanted to come in for some lemonade, but I told her I had to go back to Miss Ava's. I had told her I wouldn't be gone long.

"If you'll come over tomorrow," Michelle said, "I'll draw your picture. You have a pretty face."

I didn't think I had a pretty face, but if Michelle did, that was nice. I told her I would see her tomorrow. Then I went back to Miss Ava's.

I wanted to say that I went home, but I wasn't sure that I was allowed to call Miss Ava's big house home. It was where I was staying, but I didn't know how long, or—if I had to leave there—where I'd go. All I knew was that I was a long way from Al, and Miss Erin was taking care of me. It was a blessing as long as it lasted.

When Miss Erin came in to tell me goodnight, I told her about meeting Michelle and that I wanted to go back to see her. She said Michelle was a lovely girl, and she was glad we had gotten together. She said that if I wanted to ask Michelle to come to their house, I could. Then she kissed me on the forehead and turned off the light.

The next day I went back to Michelle's. She was already out in the swing with her drawing pad, the wheelchair parked at the end of the swing. She smiled when she saw me turn the corner.

"I was hoping you'd come. I don't get to draw people often. Mama and Daddy are too busy to sit for me for long, and Sam just doesn't want to."

"Sam?"

"Sam's our cat. I've been trying to draw Sam for a year. He sleeps in the window seat in the sun, at least until I get ready to draw him. Then he gets up and runs off. Why don't you pull my chair around, and you can sit in that."

I rolled the wheelchair around in front of the swing and sat down in it. I felt the seat sag a little. A wheelchair felt different from a regular chair. Michelle had to sit in this every day. She hadn't said why she couldn't walk. She just seemed to want to talk about what she was doing or was going to do. I decided that was a good idea. I wouldn't tell her about Mama and Al, either.

"Turn your head a little bit that way," she said, "like you're looking at something way far off."

So I turned my head and looked across the yard at the place where the green trees connected with the blue sky. I wondered how long Michelle had used the wheelchair, what it felt like to have to get around with the metal arms next to your side all the time. I couldn't blame her for wanting to sit in the swing. The wheelchair felt like it wanted to wrap around me.

We didn't talk much. It didn't feel like we needed to. Michelle drew, and I tried to look like I was looking at something far off. I couldn't remember being quiet just because I wanted to. A lot of times I'd been quiet because I had to because I didn't want to make Al mad. This was a peaceful kind of quiet. I was a little startled when, in about twenty minutes, Michelle said she was finished. She handed me the pad so that I could look at the picture. I could tell it was me, but I thought the face was prettier than mine really was. Maybe people draw things like they want them to look.

"That's nice," I said. I handed the pad back to her. She tore the paper from her pad and gave it to me.

"You can have this one," she said. "I'll do another one for me to keep."

I took the picture home with me that day and put it in the room where I was sleeping. I studied the face that was supposed to be mine but didn't seem to be. I wondered if I could grow up to be that pretty, that calm. The person in the picture didn't seem to be afraid. That's the way I wanted to be.

The day after I got the picture, I went to Michelle's and asked her if she wanted to come to Miss Ava's. Miss Ava had made a big pitcher of lemonade that morning, and she'd said that if Michelle came over, she'd make tomato sandwiches. We could have what she called a "luncheon."

I sat on the front steps waiting for Michelle. I'd never gone to a luncheon before, much less had one at my house. I guessed you just ate and talked. I was thinking about things to talk about when Michelle rolled up the front sidewalk. She rolled right up to the front steps and stopped. We hadn't thought about how we were going to get her in the house. Our house didn't have a ramp like Michelle's did.

There were only two steps leading up to the little porch, but that was two more than Michelle could climb. I decided I needed some help. I went and got Miss Ava, and she called for Miss Erin. Miss Ava got on one side, Miss Erin on the other, and I grabbed the handles on the back. It took some grunting, but between the three of us, we managed to lift Michelle's wheelchair up the two steps until the front wheels were on the porch. Then Miss Erin just pushed her in the door.

I think Michelle might have been a little embarrassed while we were fussing over her, but as soon as she got into the house where she could roll around on her own she was smiling again. She rolled up and handed me a rolled-up sheet of paper.

"It's Sam," she said. "At least as much as I could do before he ran off."

The picture showed a cat curled up on a window seat. The window and the front of the cat looked real. The back of the cat didn't have much. I guessed that was what she was drawing when Sam ran off.

"This is nice," I said. "Maybe you can finish it later."

She shook her head. "Seems like if I go back to something, it's changed. Or maybe I've changed. I'll just do another one."

Miss Ava called us into the kitchen. She'd put a tablecloth on the table, two big glasses of lemonade, and a plate with a stack of tomato sandwiches in the middle. She'd folded up cloth napkins and put them into some wooden things that looked like baby bracelets. She'd told me that those were napkin rings, and she and Miss Erin had shown me how to take the napkin out of the rings and spread it in my lap.

Michelle and I took sips of lemonade and put sandwiches on our plate. It seemed like there were a lot more tomato sandwiches there than two people could eat. I just concentrated on trying to get the sandwich to my mouth without tomato juice and mayonnaise running down my arm.

Michelle put her sandwich down and looked straight at me. "You haven't asked me why I can't walk," she said. "Almost everybody asks me that like it's the most important thing about me."

"I didn't know if you wanted to talk about it. I know there are some things I don't like to talk about."

She took another bite of her sandwich, staring at the plate as she chewed.

"I've never really walked," she said. "Daddy says I was just taking my first steps when they found that I had a tumor on my spine. They had to take out the tumor, and when they did, they had to cut my spine. That meant that I'd never walk. But I get around pretty good. I guess that's why I learned to draw. Can't dance."

I guess I must have looked blank or something because she reached over and punched me on the arm.

"That was a joke. Sort of."

We had our tomato sandwiches and lemonade, and we talked about the things we liked to do. Both of us liked to read a lot. Neither one of us knew what we wanted to be when we grew up, except Michelle thought she'd like to be an artist if she was good enough.

I told her that I thought that she would be plenty good enough.

"You come over to my house, and I'll show you some pictures in my books. They were drawn by real artists, and I guess I've learned enough now to know how much better they are than I am."

"But they're a lot older than you are."

"Most of them are dead. You can't get any older than that. But they did great pictures. I'd like to be able to leave something like that, something everybody would remember me by."

"I've never thought about being remembered. I guess I was just trying to go from one day to the next."

Michelle looked real solemn.

"That's sad. You need to start thinking about something that people will remember you for. Maybe you could be a writer or a movie star. Or maybe you could be a famous medical missionary. I think everybody ought to be remembered."

I told her I'd think about it. Maybe I could come up with something, but I knew that mostly I'd think about starting to school in September.

The rest of the summer went pretty much the same way. I would go to Michelle's. Sometimes she would draw another picture of me. And she would come to Miss Ava's. Miss Erin had gotten out her old record player and a bunch of records. We'd listen to records. Sometimes I'd push Michelle around in a kind of dance.

Once Miss Erin took us to the museum in Raleigh. We had to push Michelle up the long hill to the museum, but once we got there, she was able to roll around all the exhibits. I saw a lot of stuff that I'd never seen before.

Toward the end of the summer, Miss Erin started going to the doctor nearly every week. She didn't get out much; she'd just read or sit and talk to Miss Ava when she was fixing dinner. She didn't look much different, and she still smiled a lot, but I could tell something was happening.

One day I went over to Michelle's, and she was sitting in her chair outside the front door waiting for me. As soon as she saw me, she started rolling down the sidewalk.

"I want to go somewhere," she said.

"Okay," I said. "Where do you want to go?"

She shook her head.

"I don't know. I just want to go somewhere, somewhere I haven't been before. I'm just tired of being here."

I don't think I'd ever heard Michelle complain about anything. I didn't complain much; I knew it didn't do any good, and with Al, it would just get you hit, but Michelle complained less than I did, even though she couldn't walk. In fact, a lot of times I told myself that I could deal with things like Ann Carol's ignoring me if Michelle could deal with having legs that didn't work.

I sat down on the sidewalk beside her chair and tried to look thoughtful.

"What are you doing?" she asked.

"I'm trying to think of somewhere to go. I don't know much about Smithfield, not near as much as you do."

She looked at me like I was not too smart.

"The only places I've ever been have been with my momma and daddy or with somebody like Miss Erin. I have never even been downtown by myself. I'm thirteen years old." She stared hard out in the yard at nothing. "That's just not right."

Suddenly she clapped her hands. When she turned around to me, she had a big smile on her face.

"I know where we can go. We can go to the river."

I'd never been to the river, but I knew we crossed it when we were going to some places in the car. It seemed like it was pretty far away. Maybe further than we ought to go. But Michelle looked like she was trying to jump up and down in her chair she was so excited, so I didn't say anything.

"I'll just tell her we're going for a walk," she said. "That won't be a lie either. I just won't say where."

Miss Erin and I had talked about the difference between telling a lie and not telling the truth. According to Miss Erin, there wasn't much. I wanted to tell Michelle that, but I didn't want to make her sad when she was so excited. I just stood there and looked at her. It wasn't like we were going to break a law or anything. And if we got back soon, nobody would ever know that we'd been. I decided that if that was where Michelle wanted to go, I ought to go, too.

"Okay," I said. "But we can't be gone long. I don't want to make Miss Ava and Miss Erin worry about me."

"We won't," Michelle said. "We'll be back before they even know we were gone."

I ran back to Miss Ava's to tell them. When I got back to Michelle's house, she was sitting in her chair on the front sidewalk with her drawing pad in her lap.

"It'll help if you'll carry this," she said, handing the pad to me. I could see her pencils in the little bag that was hanging on the side of the chair.

She started wheeling along the sidewalk. I walked along beside her, the big pad under my arm.

"What'd your mama say?"

"She said 'OK,' and that I shouldn't be gone too long."

We walked out of Michelle's neighborhood and just kept walking; at least I was walking, and Michelle was rolling herself along. It wasn't long before the houses started getting smaller, and the yards weren't as nice. Then, a little way after that, the sidewalk just stopped.

There were a lot of cars on the street. The street was narrow, and the wind from the cars pushed us as they went by. The little dirt path that ran beside the street didn't look wide enough for Michelle's chair.

"You think we ought to go back?" I thought we should.

Michelle shook her head.

"The path will be good enough. The river's not too much further that way."

Then she bumped off the sidewalk and down the path. The further we went, the more it looked like where I came from, just flatter. The little houses beside the road almost didn't have grass, and the cars were parked all around the front yard. A lot of them looked like they hadn't been cranked in a while, and some of them didn't have tires. Michelle bumped along the dirt path, and sometimes I'd give her a shove to get her over a hump. The wind from the cars on the road felt stronger and stronger.

We came over a little hill, and I could see the river bridge at the bottom of it. I don't know how far we'd come, but we'd made it to the river. I asked Michelle if she wanted to turn around and go back.

"No, I thought I'd draw some. There's got to be some things here I've never drawn. Let's see how close we can get to the river."

I walked down to the bridge. Right beside the bridge, there was a path about twice as wide as Michelle's wheelchair that went down the bank to the edge of the river. It was dirt and rock, with the concrete of the bridge on one side and trees right up to the edge of it on the other. Roots crossed the path like big arms reaching to the other side. It wouldn't be hard to walk down, but it'd be a hundred bumps to the bottom in a wheelchair. I didn't see how Michelle could get down, and if she did, I didn't see how I could push her back up.

"I don't know. Why don't you draw something up here? Or maybe you could draw me sitting on the bridge."

Michelle wheeled herself around so that she was looking right at me.

"Do you know what it feels like to have people always telling what you can't do and where you can't go?"

I did. Al was always telling me what I couldn't do and what I had to do and where I couldn't go, like to school, but looking at the fierceness in Michelle's eyes, I didn't think it was a good time to bring it up.

"I'm just sick of it. For once in my life, I want to decide to go somewhere and go, just because I want to. If God was going to give me legs that didn't work, it would have been nice if he'd given me a mind that wanted to sit still."

Then she turned and headed to the path.

"Either you can help me down it, or I'll go down by myself."

I ran up behind her, grabbed the handles of her wheelchair, and we began inching our way down to the river, edging over the roots. If I sort of pushed the chair from one side of the path to the other, it wasn't so hard, and it only took us three or four minutes to get from the road to the river bank.

It was prettier down by the water. The river wasn't very wide, and it ran so slow that you couldn't tell it was running at all. Big ferns grew all along the bank, and the sun came through the tree branches to glittering spots like diamonds on the water. Right at the edge of the river, I found a flat spot to park Michelle's chair.

Michelle sat there, looking up and down the river. I guess she was looking for something to draw. I found an old log and stretched out on it. I didn't know how much I missed this kind of quiet. The only noise was the river and sometimes a car going over the bridge. But since this wasn't the main bridge, that didn't happen often.

I must have gone to sleep on the log because Michelle was tapping me on the shoulder and showing me her picture. There was an old boat hung up in the middle of the river. She had drawn the shiny streaks on the water and the shadows on the rock. When I sat up and looked out at the river, it looked almost exactly like her drawing.

"What time is it?" I asked.

"I don't know. I guess I got so involved in my drawing I lost track of time."

I looked up, but I couldn't see enough of the sun through the trees to tell whether it was morning or afternoon or November. I just knew we had been here long enough for Michelle to draw her picture. Probably too long.

"We better get going," I said. "Your mama'll be worried about you." I didn't say anything about Miss Erin or Miss Ava. I didn't know if they'd be worried or if they'd be mad. Either way, they might decide having me around was just too much trouble.

I grabbed the handles to Michelle's chair and started pushing her toward the path going up the bank. She grabbed hold of the arms of the chair.

"Slow down. You're going to bounce me right out," she said.

I slowed down. There wasn't much use of me getting back to Michelle's house in a hurry if I didn't have Michelle with me. I shoved the chair a little one way, then a little the other, the same way we had come down the bank, but now the chair with Michelle in it was a whole lot heavier. It took a while, maybe five minutes, to get halfway up the bank, and I had to stop and catch my breath.

"Maybe it'd be easier if I got out of the chair, and you just pulled me up the bank," Michelle said. "Then, you could come back and get the chair."

I thought about it, but I couldn't think of any way of pulling Michelle up the bank that wouldn't bang her up. I couldn't carry her. I couldn't even keep her off the ground very well. I just sat there, breathing hard, trying to think of some way to get Michelle and her chair back to the road. From where I was sitting, it looked a lot further than it had when we were coming down.

We started out again, me pushing and Michelle lunging forward every time we had to go over a bump. We were sweating like a couple of hogs, and neither one of us was dressed right for what we were doing. For the first time since I had come to Smithfield, I wished I had some of my old clothes. It wouldn't have mattered if I'd gotten them dirty or ruined them. But Miss Ava and Miss Erin were teaching me to dress like what they called a lady. I guess ladies didn't go down to the river with a friend in a wheelchair.

I was thinking about telling Michelle that we ought to plan better next time she wanted to go somewhere, but I couldn't say much because I needed all the wind I had to push her up the riverbank.

We had gotten near the top when we hit a big root running across the path. It just reached out and grabbed the chair, stopping it so hard that Michelle almost fell out. I shoved, and Michelle pulled forward in her chair as hard as she could, but we couldn't get the wheels over the root. I pushed down on the handles to get the front wheels over the root, but all that happened was that the back wheels hit the root and stopped.

I took a step back to get under the handles; I was going to lift the back wheels up and over, but as soon as I did, my feet slipped out from under me. I fell flat on the ground, pulling one side of the chair with me. Michelle screamed. She grabbed at the chair, then at me. She landed on the ground and started rolling down the hill, bumping against the roots and rocks, the chair sliding down behind her. The chair stopped about halfway down, but Michelle kept rolling to the bottom. I jumped up and ran down the hill after her.

When I got to the bottom, Michelle was lying up against a rock, and her head was all bloody. She was crying.

I pulled out my shirttail and used it to clean the dirt and blood off of her face. It was bleeding a lot, but I couldn't tell how big the cut was. She grabbed my hand. She was still crying.

"You think you broke anything?" I asked her. Her legs looked sort of funny, but sometimes they just did.

She shook her head. Her grip on my hand got tighter, and when I tried to ease it away, she pulled me back toward her.

"Let me go up and get your chair. We need to get you home so your mama can clean up this little place on your head."

Michelle just held on to my hand, shaking her head.

"Don't leave me," she said. I almost couldn't understand her because she was crying so hard.

"I'm just going up the path and get your chair; then we'll go home. You're going to be just fine."

She finally turned loose of my arm, and I ran up the path to the chair. But when I started to push it down the path, I saw one of the wheels was bent. It didn't look like that chair was going anywhere. I left it sitting beside the path and walked back down to Michelle.

She was sitting up and had almost quit crying when I got back to her. She was holding her shirttail against her head to make it quit bleeding. Still, she didn't look too good, and I was going to have to figure out how to get her back home. Without her chair.

"Did you see my drawing pad?"

I hadn't really thought about her drawing pad and her pencils. They were up there on the path, somewhere between where she started falling and where she ended up, but I didn't think that was one of our biggest problems. I just shook my head.

"I'm going to have to go get some help," I said. "Maybe I can stop somebody up on the road."

"I don't want you to leave me, Doris. I'm afraid."

I guess afraid is sort of the difference between what you're used to and where you are, because I wasn't afraid. I was afraid of Al. I knew he would hurt me. And I was afraid of Miss Erin and Miss Ava making me go away because they didn't want me around. But I wasn't really afraid of being here at the bottom of the path by the river. I figured that either I'd figure some way to get us out or somebody else would. So I just sat there with Michelle for a few minutes, making sure that the bleeding from the cut on her head had stopped. Turned out it wasn't all that big, but she was going to have a knot there. I started thinking again about how I was going to get us home. There was no way she was going to roll home in that chair, and I couldn't carry her. That didn't leave a lot of choices. I was going to have to find some help.

I pulled her over to a tree so she could lean back. Then I told her I was going to look for her pencils and pad. That was mostly true. I was going up the path, and I'd look for her stuff as I went, but what I really wanted to do was get up to the road and see if I could stop a car. In the back of my mind, I was hoping that the car I stopped had a nice person in it.

The drawing pad was about halfway up the path, off to the side, and the box of pencils was just a little further. I grabbed them up as I went. When I got to the road, I looked both ways to see if a car was coming. I wished the road was busier.

One old pickup came along, and I put the pencils and pads down so I could wave both arms. Either the old man driving the pickup didn't see me or didn't want to have anything to do with me. He just kept going. I could hear Michelle calling me from the bottom of the path.

Finally, I heard a car coming, and when it came around the curve, I saw it had "Smithfield Police Department" written on the side of it and the lights on top of it. I whooshed my breath out. Policemen were paid to be nice. I waved my arms, and the police car pulled up beside me. Inside was a policeman who didn't look a whole lot older than me. His hair was cut flat on top and was about as long as the bristles on my hairbrush. He looked like he was going to be nice. Not mean, anyway.

"You Doris?" the policeman asked.

How did he know that? I nodded my head.

"Where's Michelle?"

"She's down at the bottom of the path. Her chair's broken, and I couldn't get her up."

The policeman pulled off the road. I saw him saying something into his radio microphone. Then he got out.

"I was just telling my dispatcher to call your folks and tell them you're okay. Michelle is okay, isn't she?"

"She's okay. She's got a little cut on her head, but it's not bleeding anymore."

We started walking down the path. I brought Michelle's pad and pencils with me. The policeman told me that they'd been looking for us for about an hour, after Miss Erin called and said she was afraid something had happened to us. He seemed sort of ashamed that it took a whole police department an hour to find us, since he said it shouldn't have been that hard to find two little girls, especially when one of them was in a wheelchair.

He picked Michelle up and carried her up the path. I dragged the wheelchair behind him. He put us in the back seat and the wheelchair in the trunk and started to take us home.

Then I started worrying again about Miss Erin and Miss Ava. Miss Erin did call the police, and that was a good thing. She did want somebody to find me, or maybe she just did it because Michelle's mama had thought I had done something to Michelle.

I wondered where I would go if Miss Erin and Miss Ava wouldn't have me anymore. The only thing I could think to say to them was that it was Michelle's idea, and Michelle was the last person in the world that you think would get you into trouble. I wasn't sure what good saying that would do.

It was just a couple of minutes before the police car pulled up in front of Michelle's house. Miss Erin and Miss Ava were standing in the front yard with Michelle's mama and daddy. When the policeman opened the back door of the car, her daddy rushed up and picked Michelle up. I heard her say, "I'm sorry, Daddy." He didn't say anything. He just stood there holding her. I got out of the car, not knowing what to say or what to do. Suddenly Miss Erin grabbed me up and pulled me tight against her. I thought I might crack, then I felt something wet on my neck, and I realized she was crying.

"I was afraid I had lost you," she said, her voice sort of muffled because she was holding me so tight. "I was so afraid."

Miss Ava came up and put her arms around both of us, telling Miss Erin that everything was alright, nobody was hurt, and everybody was back home. She thanked the policeman for bringing us back, said something to Michelle's folks, then we walked back to their house. Miss Erin kept her arm around my shoulders all the way back like she was afraid if she turned loose I would disappear again.

That was the biggest thing that happened to me all that summer. It wasn't that we went somewhere that we'd never been before. Or that we had to be found by the police. It was that on that walk home, for the very first time in my life, I knew I really belonged somewhere and that the people there wanted me to be with them. I didn't cry, at least not until I got up into my room. Maybe it was the idea that it was my room, and I didn't have to wonder about that anymore.

A few weeks later, I started to school. Michelle and I walked to school together unless it was raining. I made some friends.

Ann Carol and her friends didn't show any interest in me, but I didn't care.

Not long after school started, Miss Erin began going to the doctor more often. Then she'd come home and lie down. Sometimes I'd sit beside her on the bed, and we'd look through magazines together. Miss Ava would stay with us sometimes. I could tell that Miss Erin wasn't feeling good, but she'd never admit it. She'd always say she felt fine, but was just a little tired. I noticed that she hugged me a lot when I got home from school. I always hugged her back.

Miss Erin didn't go to the hospital. She just passed one night, and when Miss Ava got up the next morning to fix our breakfast, she found her. Miss Ava made some phone calls; then she took me into the living room to wait for the men from the funeral home.

We sat on the sofa, Miss Ava with her arm around me, talking about Miss Erin. I was crying.

"I don't have a lot of crying left to do," she said. "When Erin had to start going to the doctor every week, we knew that it wouldn't be long. Then I cried every night."

She put her fingers under my chin and pulled my face up so I could see her.

"But, you know, Erin wasn't sad. I think she was happy until the very last breath she drew. She didn't want to go away, and she didn't want to make us sad, but she told me that she'd done two important things, the most important things she'd done in her whole life. She'd found you, and she'd learned to love me. And, Lord knows, I loved her."

The men from the funeral home came and took Miss Erin. We just sat on the sofa and watched them wheel her out the door on that spidery table thing that they had brought. I'd already started missing her.

The house started filling up with people, almost all of them carrying a dish of something. Michelle's mother and daddy brought Michelle over, and we went into a bedroom so I could talk to Michelle and cry some more. It seemed like there were people in the house almost all the time for the next two days, until the day of the funeral. After the funeral, it felt good to come home with just Miss Ava and me. She fixed us a glass of tea, and we sat at the kitchen table.

"You know," she said. "In all the talking Erin and I have done in the last few months, I've decided that there are a lot of things worse than dying. There's being alone and not having anybody to love you."

I nodded. I knew about that.

"But I think there's something a whole lot worse than that – not loving the people you should the way you should. I think not being loved is probably not the person's fault. It might be, or it might not. But I don't think God would blame us for not being loved. But not loving, that's a whole different thing. I think we have to take responsibility for not loving, and I think God's going to hold us responsible. Erin coming back here, even for a little while, was a blessing for me because I got to learn to love her like I should."

She didn't really cry. In fact, she was smiling a little bit, but the tears brimmed over her eyelids and rolled down her cheeks. Then she walked around the table, knelt beside me, and hugged me close to her. For a while, we just sat there, both of us with tears, remembering Miss Erin.

That night, when I was in my room by myself, I thought a lot about what Miss Ava had said. I started keeping a little notebook, and I wrote down a list of people I had loved and would love. There was Mama, and Miss Erin, and Miss Ava, and Michelle, and maybe Michelle's mama and daddy, who were always very nice to me, and two or three others. Every night I would look at the list and sometimes add somebody else to it. I decided I wanted to love everybody I was supposed to, and maybe even some of those that I didn't have any reason to. Like Miss Erin did.

AVA

I cried when Doris left for college.

I suppose mothers are supposed to cry when their daughters leave home. However, Doris isn't my daughter, and I didn't cry at all when my own daughter left. In fact, I would have rejoiced by dancing on the lawn if I hadn't thought it would embarrass my husband.

I used to say that my relationship with Erin was complicated, but I was just lying to myself and everybody I said it to. It was simple. I had the love of my life until she was born; then, I had to share him. I hated that. I hated the minutes that Erin took James away from me. I hated the attention that he showed her. I resented every pat or kiss that he gave her from the time she was a baby.

I just didn't know it. I thought I loved my daughter. I changed her and bathed her, and made sure she got safe food to eat. When she got older, I hauled her to ballet classes, sat through ball games just to watch her cheer, and did my share of bragging when I was having lunch with my friends.

My beautiful, intelligent, talented Erin. Whom I resented until the day that her father died. And she knew it, even when I didn't.

If it hadn't been for Doris, I wouldn't have had nearly a year to try to make it up to Erin. It was because of Doris that she came home, more to give Doris a place to live than to give herself a place to die. But I'm very grateful for that time, because we were finally together without me putting James between us, a time when I could really appreciate who she was and be proud of what James and I had accomplished together.

Erin and I buried James. We stood by the grave, two separate islands of grief, not looking at each other, not touching, and hardly speaking. The preacher said a few words, enclosing us in them as a family, and then he prayed. I just stared at the grave.

Before Erin left the next day, I had a different vision of Erin. She wasn't the one who siphoned off the affection and attention that James should have been giving me. Now, she was the only way James could continue to live. I knew that If Erin didn't get married and have children, there would soon be nobody to remember James, and the single most important light in my life would go completely out.

I suppose the problem began when I was about thirteen. Whether it was the books I read or just because I was drowning in newly manufactured hormones, I convinced myself that there was one true love waiting for me somewhere. But only one, and I couldn't settle for someone else. It was a strange but very rigid belief, and because of it, I approached boys the same way my mother approached apples in the grocery store.

My mother was forever searching for the perfect apple. She would stand there, sometimes for ten or fifteen minutes, picking an apple up, examining it closely, and then putting it back.

All through high school, I did the same thing with boys. Because I was passably pretty, a reasonable dancer, and had learned to flirt at an early age, boys were attracted to me. Many were called, but none were chosen. I was one of the few girls in my class who went all the way through high school without a steady boyfriend. I was told that by my senior year I had a reputation for being cold. I wasn't. I just hadn't found that one who was meant for me.

That changed right after I got to the University. We were at a party at some sorority house, and I was huddled with a group of my new friends, trying to talk over the other conversations and the music booming out of the big speakers. Across the room, I saw one man who stood out from all the boys around him. He was the most handsome man I'd ever seen. Thick black hair, just a bit too long to get by my daddy. More than six feet tall, tanned, and with amazing white teeth. Nobody I had dated in high school even came close.

I asked the girl next to me who he was, and she giggled.

"Everybody wants to know who he is," she said. "Can't imagine why." And she giggled again. "His name is James," she said, "never Jim."

I stood there for a few minutes, guarded by my circle of friends, wondering whether this was the one I had been waiting for. I told myself that I was being silly, that I'd never even spoken to him, that he probably had a girlfriend.

Then he came over to our corner of the room.

When my friend introduced us, he smiled at me and asked where I came from, what I was going to major in, what I wanted to do. He seemed more interested in me than in himself. I wasn't used to that either.

James and I started dating, and it wasn't long before we moved in together. My parents thought I was still living in the dorm, and according to the school records, I was, but most of what I had and most of the nights I spent were in James' off-campus apartment. They wouldn't have understood it, but since this was the seventies, nobody on campus cared.

He didn't like to talk about himself, but I learned some things about him. He'd wanted to be a preacher, but while he was in high school, he decided that the decision wasn't based on a real calling but more of a desire to stand in front of people and talk about things he thought were important. He found that he could do the same thing on the debate team. He said that didn't make him any less a Christian, but admitting it did make him less of a hypocrite.

He had a real talent for making people feel special. He would bring me a rose or a whole bunch of roses and say it was just because he was thinking of me. When he met a stranger, he would look at the stranger closely, hanging on every word, and when the conversation was over, he would know that person's name and probably a large part of the life story. It was important to him. That was just one more part of him that I was proud of, just as I was proud of his good grades and the fact that others always seemed to look up to him. It was an important part of what made James the person he was.

I took James home with me one weekend to meet my parents. My father was taken by his straight-forward handshake and good manners. My mother didn't need to get that close to him to know that I had finally found the right apple.

One night, not long after our trip to see my family, we were in his apartment. We had been studying, but now we were just stretched out on the sofa, my head on his shoulder, listening to Bob Dylan.

He whispered something into my ear, but I didn't understand it. I just raised my eyebrows.

"Marry me?" he said, this time out loud.

I smiled, and I nodded and buried my head a little deeper into that perfect fitting place between his shoulder and his chest.

On the day we decided that we were going to get married—although I hadn't had any doubt—I knew that whatever my life was going to be, it would be wonderful with James. And that's the way I kept thinking, through all the engagement parties and showers, the wedding, and the first three years of our married life.

There was still enough of the old fashioned southern girl in me to see and follow the track laid out in front of me. Get married, have children, keep a clean house, and be a credit to James, whatever he decided to do.

He had decided to be a banker, not what I would have picked out for him. I thought he was capable of a lot more than that, and I said it one time. He told me that what he did was not who he was and that the bank would give us a good living. He didn't mind putting on a coat and tie every day and sitting behind a desk. It was a big bank, and there was a lot of room for him to grow.

He said that he would grow as much as they would let him so long as he didn't have to leave Smithfield. That's where he wanted to stay. His family had been there for nearly two hundred years, and except for his four years at college, he'd never lived anywhere else. Smithfield was as connected to him as his arm or his leg.

For the most part, I accepted it. I didn't understand it, but if Smithfield was part of James, I would learn to love it, too. And that's the way it was, except for one time. He'd been with the bank for nearly fifteen years, and they had offered him a promotion to Vice President for something. It meant a big raise, and in my mind, I could see James rising to be president of the bank. And I would be the wife of the president. The only problem was that we would have had to move to Greensboro. We were in our bedroom, arguing in whispering voices because Erin was sleeping just down the hall.

"This is a wonderful opportunity," I said. I knew it was for me, and I thought it was for him.

"No, it's a move to Greensboro. We can do very well without moving to Greensboro."

He walked over to the window.

"Besides," he said, "I've already told them that I wouldn't take it."

I sat down on the bed, trying to make sense out of the fact that he had told me about it, but not until it didn't matter. The decision was already made.

"You didn't think we should have talked about this, that I should have something to say about where I live?"

"It's not just about where you live. It's about where we live. It's about where we raise our family."

He turned around.

"Is this so bad that you want to leave it?"

We argued that night, but my heart wasn't really in it because I knew James was going to stay in Smithfield, and I knew I wanted to be wherever he was.

James finally did make vice president, and they fixed it so he could be vice president from Smithfield. He traveled some, but mostly he was home every night. He made enough money that we could be part of a fairly small group of very prosperous people.

I don't know when I started being so jealous. Maybe it was one night when Erin was a baby, and I woke up and reached out to James, and he wasn't there. I got up and found him in Erin's room, sitting in a chair, just looking into her crib with a big smile on his face. The only other time I had seen that smile was when he was looking at me. I crept back to my bed.

It's possible that neither Erin nor I realized that all mothers and daughters didn't have the kind of relationship we had, but James did. At first, he thought he could fix it. When Erin was a toddler, he'd have her bring me a flower or a picture. I'd take it and then go back to whatever I was doing. Finally, he decided he couldn't change it and resigned himself to live with it.

In a way, that made James live two lives—perhaps three. The bank. My husband. Erin's father. All separate. And at least two of them nearly all-consuming. He seemed like he gave everything he had to each of us.

By the time Erin was three or four, he had learned that I didn't want to talk about her or what she had done. We did, of course, exchange information, but there was no dreaming involving Erin. At least on my part. James, bless his heart, learned to compartmentalize his dreams just like he did his life. And until Erin became a teenager, that seemed to work.

Then one night, it broke down. The evening had started out noisily. Erin was going out with her friends, and for whatever reason, I had decided to play my concerned mother role. I'm not sure that I really cared where Erin was going, but I knew that a normal mother should care.

She came down the steps, wearing jeans that were too tight and a top that showed inches of skin above them.

"Where are you going?" I managed not to say, "dressed like that." All the girls dressed like that.

She just kept walking. I stood up.

"I asked you where you were going. Who are you going with? When will you be back?" My voice got a little higher and a little shriller with each question.

Finally, she just stopped and looked at me. "I'm going out. I'm going out with my friends. And what the hell do you care anyway?"

I started screaming at her. I don't remember what I said, but I do remember she looked at me very calmly. I have never felt so helpless in my life. I couldn't even provoke teenage anger in my daughter. Finally, I quit yelling and went into my bedroom—James' and my bedroom—and fell across the bed.

When James came home from work, he asked where Erin was. I said I didn't know. He went upstairs to change his clothes.

Hours later, when it was time for Erin to be home, James started looking at his watch every few minutes. Then he went to the door and looked out. I sat there and stared at the big-haired blond newscaster. I'd never seen James so agitated. He was usually the picture of calm, always making molehills out of mountains. But the later it got, the quicker he paced, and the more he muttered to himself. I heard him go into the kitchen and dial the phone.

"Fred, have you heard anything from the kids? They were supposed to be home an hour ago."

Then silence. I don't know what Fred said, but the next thing James said was: "OK. You check the hospitals. I'll call the police."

I wasn't sure what to do. Evidently, I was supposed to be upset, wanting to do something, but I didn't. It's difficult when you're supposed to be playing a role and don't understand your motivation. What does a loving mother do when her daughter is out? Does she get angry, thinking that teenagers are always flouting the rules? Does she get worried, thinking that the daughter and all of her friends are perhaps dead or bleeding in a wrecked car? The script was unclear. I just sat there.

I heard James dialing again, presumably the police. He must have been facing the other way because his words were muffled, just hurried bits of sound separated by periods of silence. Finally, he hung up the phone and walked slowly into the den.

"The police don't know anything," he said. "Nobody's reported a wreck."

He dropped into his chair, staring straight ahead. I felt very sorry for him.

It was nearly two hours later when we got a call from the police. The car that Erin and her friends were in had gone off the road, down an embankment, and had stayed there—unseen—for several hours. When the police finally got to the car, one of the passengers was dead, and Erin and the driver were unconscious. The police said that they had been taken to the hospital.

We rode to the hospital in a cold silence. I could see James' jaw clenching and unclenching. He would look at me and then back at the road.

"What did you say to her?"

I shuddered. He thought that I had driven her off.

"Nothing," I said. "I asked her where she was going, and she asked me what did I care. Then she left. I don't know where she was going or what she was going to do."

He didn't say anything. He just stared at the road and drove. For the first time, I prayed that Erin would be all right. I knew that if she died, James would never forgive me.

By the time we got to the hospital, they had already sent Erin to surgery. The nurse told us that the doctor would be with us as soon as the surgery was over, that Erin had internal injuries that had to be fixed.

The hospital smelled like medicine and disinfectant. The doctors and nurses were rushing through the doors and down the halls. In one of the chairs in the corner, a young woman was crying. We just stood there in the middle of the room, like a small island in a stream of people hurrying one way or another, calling to each other, doing something purposeful.

I put my hand on James' arm. He didn't pull away, but he didn't acknowledge me either. He knew that I was there for him, not Erin. Even as I prayed that Erin would make it, God help me, at some level I was wishing that Erin would never come out of that operating room. I didn't admit it to myself then and would never admit it to anybody else, but I wondered if God hadn't figured out a way to give me back all of James.

About an hour later, the doctor came in and told us that Erin would be fine, that she was banged up, but the internal bleeding had been stopped. She'd be in the hospital for a while, but—eventually—she'd be fine.

James collapsed in his chair, his face in his hands, sobbing. I just walked over to the window and stood, staring out at the darkness, wondering why God hadn't taken advantage of this opportunity.

When Erin came home from the hospital, James paid her even more attention. He had almost lost her, and he didn't want to miss a moment now that he had her back. I moved further and further into the background.

Then she left for college. James drove her to Chapel Hill and helped her move in. But I didn't begrudge either of them that time. I knew that when he came back, once again, I would have James all to myself again.

It was like before Erin was born. We'd go out with friends. We had the house all to ourselves. We were older, but I convinced myself that we were just as much in love. Erin wrote us letters, but they were almost completely directed to James, things that they shared or had talked about, or things that she knew would make him proud. I didn't mind that. She had a pen pal; I had James.

And I had him nearly all to myself for nine wonderful years. And then, suddenly, I didn't. It was on a Thursday when his secretary called me and said that James had collapsed and had been taken to the hospital. She said that I should get over there as quickly as possible.

This was the same hospital that they took Erin to. There was the same blur of people rushing back and forth, the same noise. But they hadn't taken James to surgery. He was already dead; he had died in the ambulance on the way to the hospital from what the doctor called a massive heart attack.

He had kissed me goodbye that morning and walked out the door just as he had for nearly forty years. Still a young man at sixty-three. We had talked about taking a vacation to New England in the summer, and he'd wondered whether Erin would want to go. I told him that I doubted it. She had her job and her friends, her own life. He just nodded, kissed me, and left, and I never talked to him again.

Some of the people from the bank came to the hospital, and one of them took me home. The doctor had given me a shot of something, and I was too groggy to drive but too upset to sleep. Somebody asked if he should call Erin. I think I said yes.

I don't remember much about days after that. Erin came home, and even without James, we fell into our old pattern. The house was big enough that we weren't forced into each other, and for both of us, that was fine.

Only once the day that she came home did she approach me. She heard me crying in my—our—bedroom. She knocked on the door and stepped in.

"Can I get you something?" she asked. I just shook my head, and she stepped back out.

James' funeral was big. They closed the bank for the afternoon, and most of the people he worked with came. The church was full, and flowers covered the entire pulpit area. James lay in a mahogany casket in front of the pulpit.

People came up and touched my arm and muttered words that I didn't understand. At the other end of the same pew, Erin's friends were gathered around her. Finally, we sat down, side by side, but not touching, and the preacher got up. I saw the whole thing through tears, a scene through a dirty, smeared lens. I stood up when I was supposed to. I walked out when I was supposed to, but only because one of the men from the funeral home was there beside me. I didn't know what was going on.

After the funeral, when we got home, I went to our bedroom and collapsed on the bed, crying. I had had, I thought, my one chance at true love, and it was over. I still had too long to live.

But I managed to make living as small as possible. I went about my life—shopping, talking to friends, going to church—with my body almost totally disconnected from my emotions. Almost nobody noticed that I wasn't really there. Sally Edmondson was the exception. She showed up at my back door one afternoon, holding a pitcher.

"I need a word with you," she said. She glanced down at the pitcher. It was obviously lemonade, with slices of lemon floating in it, beads of water sliding down the sides.

I opened the door and got two glasses from the cabinet.

"About what?"

She didn't say anything. She just put some ice in the glasses and poured the lemonade. She handed me a glass.

It was a hot day, and the lemonade looked good. I took a deep swallow, and only then did I realize that the lemonade was just a little lemon and a lot of vodka.

"Drink up," she said. "You've been walking around wrapped up long enough. All that armor needs a rest."

I did drink up. I finished that glass, then another one. Before I finished the second glass, I began weeping, first with tears trickling down my cheeks, then with deep sucking sobs. Sarah put her arms around me and sat there. I don't know how long I cried, but I remember her helping me to bed. Then she left.

I wish that I could say that Sarah's lemonade brought me back to life, but it didn't. It let me pour out the grief I had backed up just to make room for some more. I would call Erin occasionally, wanting to know if she had any plans for getting married. Finally, she started avoiding my calls. I just retreated further into my memories.

If Erin hadn't come home with Doris, I would have lived that way until I died. And I wouldn't have cared.

When Erin called that morning, it was very confusing. I was surprised to hear from her. It had been weeks since I had called her and more weeks since I had spoken with her.

I tried to sound like I was glad to hear from her. At first, she was very quiet.

"How are you, Mother?" she said.

"I'm fine. It's so good to hear from you."

There was a pause.

"Could I come home for a while?"

There was no reason she shouldn't. She couldn't take any part of James from me anymore. Except for my memories, he was gone. I told her that I would be glad for her to come home and stay as long as she liked.

"I'm bringing someone with me," she said.

I felt a flash of excitement. Maybe she was going to get married.

"Her name is Doris. She's thirteen, and she needs help."

The day Erin was coming home, I was up early. By nine o'clock, I'd vacuumed her room and the guest room and put clean linens on the beds. Then I went back through the house again, moving a figurine here or setting a picture there. I wanted, I think, for her to see the house as it was when she left it. I can't imagine why I wanted that. When she left, we were barely speaking. James was gone. And I was alone.

It was, I suppose, the old world of scripts. Mothers are supposed to behave this way. Mothers are supposed to prepare joyful homecomings for their children. Mothers are supposed...

But I didn't know much about being a mother. I knew about being a wife; I had been a good and faithful wife to James for many years. I was even a pretty good friend. Alice, Brenda, and Louellen, and maybe a dozen others knew that they could count on me to do whatever I was supposed to do.

But the place in my life's work that said "mother" was almost empty, and at my age, I thought it would never be filled.

It was early afternoon when they pulled up in Erin's car. I was in the front yard, having moved, picked up, and put down almost everything I could find. So I had poured me a glass of ice tea, gone out front, and waited.

Erin got out first. She was, as she had always been, beautiful. I could see someone in the passenger seat, a little girl. Even sitting there, her head just above the bottom edge of the window, she looked thin and maybe lost. She looked at the house and yard, her eyes too large for the thin face, poised as if she would bolt at the slightest noise.

Erin walked up the sidewalk to me, and it may have been for the first time in my life that I saw my daughter as my daughter, not as competition for James or as an extension of James, but as Erin. I wrapped her in my arms, and—God's own wonder—she pulled me to her as tightly as she could.

"I'm so glad you're here," I said, holding on to her.

"Me, too."

We stood there for a moment, wound in each other, tears rolling down our cheeks. Then Erin pulled away and motioned for the little girl to join us. She got out of the car, slowly and hesitantly, and walked toward us.

"Mother, this is Doris."

Doris just made a little jerky nod of her head. Erin took Doris by the hand, bringing her over to me.

"Doris, meet my mother. You're going to like her a lot."

It might have been just a coincidence that the Sunday before Erin and Doris came home, Brenda Tate had taught our Sunday School lesson on Abraham and Sarah and the angels, the place where they say Abraham is going to have a bunch of descendants, and Sarah laughs. At her age, it was just ridiculous that she would have a child.

For a while, that's the way I felt. I was over sixty. I hadn't been successful when I was supposed to be a mother, and I didn't have any reason to believe that I'd be any more successful now. So I decided, if I couldn't be a mother, I could at least be a friend.

Erin and I would sit up late at night, after Doris had gone to bed, and talk. Sometimes we'd talk about James, sometimes about other people she'd grown up with. We would edge closer and closer to talking about us; then we would veer away to something else. I didn't know whether opening that wound would bring back more bitterness than we could overcome.

One night we were sitting in the den, sipping green tea. Erin had been to the doctor that day, and the news was no worse than we expected.

"I imagine you're going to have a good summer," the doctor had said. She didn't say how you have a good summer knowing that you'd never see winter, but Erin didn't seem to worry about it. It seemed that she'd given up worrying about dying and spent her time trying to make sure she lived as much as she could.

We talked about the doctor, about how, as nice as Dr. Ashura was, she seemed awfully matter of fact when she was telling somebody that not only were their days numbered, but the number was very small.

Erin mimicked the doctor's clipped Indian accent. Then she stopped.

"I shouldn't do that," she said. "Dr. Ashura is a good doctor, and she knows she can't change the outcome. She's just trying to do what she can do."

I nodded. I wanted to say that I wish she could do more, that I could do more, but we'd already had that conversation. I didn't want to create more regrets.

We just sat there, then Erin said, "He was big enough for both of us, you know?"

For a minute, I didn't know what she was talking about. Then I knew that "he" was James and that she had gone into what I thought was the forbidden zone.

"What do you mean?"

"There was enough of Daddy for both of us. We didn't have to compete."

I nodded. "I guess. But for some reason, I felt like every bit of him that he devoted to you was taken from me. Sounds crazy, I suppose."

"No. Wrong, probably, but not crazy. By the time I was in the first grade, I felt the same way. I wanted to be the center of his life, and if that left you wandering around like an orphan moon, I didn't care."

She came over and sat down next to me.

"You didn't do anything to me that I didn't do to you. I was a lousy daughter, and I am sorry."

I started to protest that she wasn't a lousy daughter, that I had been a terrible mother, but before any of that could come out, it struck me. We were lousy. We had managed to take the relationship that all the magazines celebrated as the most biologically bound and mangle it beyond all recognition right up to the time that one of us, the wrong one, was about to die. And for some reason, I began to laugh. Erin laughed. And the sheer absurdity of what I had spent most of my life and she had spent all of her life doing washed over us.

There was nothing really funny, but we both laughed hysterically.

It took several minutes for us to stop. I wiped my eyes and caught my breath.

"Yes, you were a lousy daughter," I said. "And I was a lousy mother. I don't think it was bad that we both wanted the same thing. I guess we were both just selfish; we wanted all of him."

She nodded and picked up her teacup. She raised it in a toast.

"Here's to him and our memories of him. And more than that, here's to having a little time for us."

I very carefully clinked my china teacup against hers.

Erin did have a good summer. She and I taught Doris how to shop for clothes, how to order from large, over-priced menus, and how to enjoy the day. Doris gained a little weight, and the flicker of fear that had so frequently crossed her face came not nearly so often.

Erin and I talked late into the night. There were no forbidden zones, no sheltered resentments. We both had regrets, but we knew that there was not enough time for them. We talked a lot about Doris' future. In her half-dozen years working, Erin had saved some money; she wanted to leave it all to Doris.

"I mean, if you don't mind," she said. "But you're my only real blood relative. It might be better if I left it to you."

"And what would I do with it? I've got everything I need, plus some. Leave it to Doris. I will, too. That ought to hold her for a while."

We spent some time speculating about what Doris might do with a fairly large pile of money and no adults to tell her what to do with it. Expensive cars. Boy toys. Diamonds and furs. Then Erin quit laughing.

"Please don't leave her too soon. There's too much she needs to learn."

I nodded, knowing that I couldn't make any promises. My daughter was leaving me; she'd lived just over thirty years. I was already past sixty.

But God has been good to me. There was a big gap between the time Erin left and the day she came back, and I hate the years I wasted pushing her away so that I could hold James closer. But, in some ways, these last eight years have been some of the happiest in my life. I got another chance to love a daughter. With Erin's blessing, I got to do with Doris so many of the things I had missed with Erin.

For one thing, we talked. A lot. Even as she grew into her teenage years, we would sit at night, discussing what happened during the day, or people that we knew, or even such deep subjects as the vicissitudes of the various ages.

"I don't understand teenage angst," I said one night.

Doris just raised her eyebrows. She was about seventeen and had grown from a skinny, frightened girl with stringy blonde hair to a much more assured, much more developed girl with really pretty blonde hair.

"What's to understand?" she said. "When you're my age, every pimple is a mountain, every breakup is a death sentence, and your entire self-worth depends on the opinion of a bunch of self-absorbed girls who prove their self-worth by trying to destroy yours. It's easy."

We laughed; then, it occurred to me that none of that, even in more realistic dimensions, applied to her. I asked her why not.

"I knew Al. When you know Al, you know how bad things can be; so you really can't get too worked up over anything that's not beating you or trying to rape you. And I'm sure not worried about what Carol Ann Jenkins thinks about me. She didn't like me when I was fourteen, she doesn't like me now, and I bet when we have our tenth class reunion, she'll think we were the best of friends. Carol Ann's world is strictly according to Carol Ann."

We just sat there for a few minutes. We had developed a companionable silence that punctuated our conversations. Neither of us thought we had to talk just to fill up the silence.

"What brought that on?" she asked.

"What?"

"The statement about teenage angst. I don't see that on our agenda for this evening."

"Point of personal privilege," I said. "Today I saw something on TV about teenage depression, and I couldn't understand it. Teenagers have their whole lives to correct the mistakes they're making now. Everything's in front of them."

"And?"

"And I, on the other hand, am almost seventy years old, and everything—nearly everything—is behind me. Sometimes I spend too much time thinking about all the things I didn't do. Time just rolled over me while I was doing things that didn't matter and not doing the things that did. I think that, if anybody's going to be depressed, it should be us old folks."

"Well, if you put it that way. But is that the way it really was?"

"I don't know. Sometimes I think so. Then sometimes, I'm just grateful that it didn't end too soon."

Doris stood up.

"I've got some studying left to do, but if it'll help, I'll make a note to throw some sort of hissy-fit tomorrow to fill your teenage angst void."

She went upstairs, and I began picking up and straightening up. All my life, I had tried to make sure everything was done before I went to bed, so I didn't wake up to unfinished business. It was a trait that James had joked about, although I think he appreciated the order it kept in our lives. But it seems that I did it only for the things that didn't matter much.

When he smoked, we never left dirty ashtrays out. There were no dishes in the sink. The newspapers were put in the trash before the next day came. It was tidy. But it wasn't important. And I still did it.

After about thirty minutes of what James used to call "piddling," I went upstairs to get ready for bed. The light was still on in Doris' room, and her radio was playing softly. I stood by her door for a moment, then walked on down the hall.

Teenagers do have time, I thought. Young adults even have time. But not only did I not have time anymore—at least the kind of time it would take to make right so many wrongs in my life—but I had lived through so many things I wished I could change.

I wished I had accepted James for what he was and hadn't, even for the shortest time, tried to push him to be something else. I wished I could have thought of us as a family, instead of Erin trying to push herself between James and me. I wished that, for all of those years, I could have loved Erin as Erin, a beautiful result of the love that James and I had.

I put on my nightgown and sat down at the dresser to brush my hair. The frilliness of the nightgown looked a little silly hanging from my sagging frame, but I liked pretty nightgowns, even though I knew nobody else would ever see them. The lacy blue straps hung over shoulders that used to be pretty, used to get kissed, but now were just bony. The bodice, more lace, lay almost flat against my chest. That didn't matter anymore.

I stared at the face in the mirror. Would it have been better for me to have changed places with either James or Erin? James would have lived and worked, and maybe even married again. He would have had a productive life without me. Erin had proved that she could live without me. She was successful on her own, building a career. Maybe she would have had a family, maybe not. She could have had a good life either way.

But that's not the way it worked out. James was gone. Erin was gone. And I was left. In the mirror, I could see the tears well up in my eyes.

I also saw Doris walking up behind me. She was dressed for bed in a pair of boy's boxer shorts and a T-shirt that had some symbol on it I didn't understand. But even without the lace and frills, she was beautiful.

She stood behind me, her hands on my shoulders.

"Why the tears?" she asked.

I just shook my head.

"Oh, come on. You don't usually let anybody see tears. Why now?"

"Because you sneaked into my room. You weren't supposed to see them."

She hugged me.

"If there's anybody in this world who should see your tears, that would be me. If there's anybody who owes her life to you, that would also be me."

She knelt by my side.

"I can't be Erin. I know that you want to go back and grab those years that you missed. But because of what Erin did and what you're doing, I have a chance. I promise you I'll make the most of it."

"I'm old," I said. "I'm old, and I don't like it."

Doris laughed. I didn't think it was nice of her to laugh at my pain or my anger, but after a moment, I couldn't help joining her.

"Life is a terminal disease, and age is just one of its symptoms," she said.

"Where did you hear that? It's much too cynical for a seventeen-year-old."

"I read it somewhere. I want to grow old. I want to spend a whole life doing things and when I get to be your age, I know I'll wish I had done some other things. But I want to be as old as you are now, or as old as you're going to be, and I'll always tell myself that whatever I do, it's because you and Erin did something for me. Somewhere, maybe a hundred years from now, there'll be somebody doing something wonderful just because of that."

Doris put her arms around me and hugged me tightly. I knew that I needed to remember that the world did not begin with me and would not end with me. I was just a link in a long chain, and I guessed that my only real job was to make sure that my link was strong enough to hold all those other links that came after me. That was better than regret.

EPILOGUE

I was in college less than two hours when I ceased to be Doris and became Dee. It wasn't a formal name change, just an off-handed comment that stuck. I was in my newly-assigned dorm room, pulling clothes out of my trunk and suitcase and putting them in drawers. I'd been told by the girl who led me to my room that since my roommate hadn't arrived, I could have the bed on either side and any of the drawers, as long as I didn't try to claim more than half of them.

I'd counted the drawers and was filling up exactly half. Then Teri came in—or rather she blew in. Teri, when I met her and in all the years that I knew her, never just entered the room. She entered laughing, talking, and taking up a lot of the space around her. In my eighteen years, I hadn't seen much, and I'd certainly never seen anybody like Teri.

"Oh, I'm really glad we're roommates," she said, before she knew anything about me, even my name. "Having a good looking roommate is a real advantage in finding boys."

I didn't think she'd have a lot of trouble. She wasn't beautiful in a conventional way. Her mouth was a little wider than it needed to be. She was slim, but not skinny. She had brown hair that fell down her back. And she had big eyes that looked as if they could take in the whole world at a glance. Most of all, there was this aura of energy that surrounded her. And it was obvious at a glance that she didn't take herself or the world too seriously. I immediately liked her.

I held out my hand. "Hi, I'm Doris," I said.

She threw her bags on the other bed, stopped, and put her finger to her cheek, apparently deep in thought.

"That won't do," she said. "Doris sounds like you're already married, attending the church circle meetings, and cooking daddy dinner. No, that won't do at all."

I laughed. "But that's my name," I said. It had always been my name, and it had done all right through high school. I'd had as many dates as I wanted.

"No, no, no," she said. "You have to remember I'm depending on you. How'd you like to be Sabrina? That's a great name. Just a little exotic. A little unusual."

"I don't feel like a Sabrina. I feel like a Doris."

"Pshaw," she poo-pooed. "That's just habit."

She sat on her bed with her suitcases, sure that the task of renaming me was more important than unpacking or even checking to see if I'd left her 50% of the drawers.

She nodded slowly.

"Okay. If you insist on being usual, you can be Dee. It's interesting, and it doesn't sound like you have to rush home to rediaper the babies. I'm going to call you Dee."

I told her that I could live with Dee. I didn't tell her that I would show up on all the class rolls as Doris, so whatever she called me probably wouldn't make a lot of difference. I was wrong. All of the forces of the college couldn't stand up to Teri. If I was Dee to her, I would soon be Dee to everyone who knew me.

Looking back on it, it seems like my life has been divided into some kind of chapters. First, there was the chapter when it was just Mama and me. I didn't remember my daddy; he was killed when I was three. Mama told me a log rolled off the truck and killed him, and the logging company gave her a little money.

She also got what she called "her little check" from the government, and Daddy had a brother who lived in Asheville who came to see us once or twice a year. He always left some groceries. He never stayed long.

Then there was the chapter when Al came to live with us.

When I was eight, Al started coming around. I was afraid of him, but Mama kept telling me that Al might be the one to take care of us.

I remember sitting by the kitchen stove, doing my homework at the table, when Mama came and sat down next to me.

"Al's going to come live here," she said. She didn't look happy about it. In fact, Mama almost never looked happy. As far back as I could remember, she was very thin with skinny arms and skinny legs, and a body that didn't fill out any part of the sack dresses she wore. She always looked worried. She looked more worried than usual that night, the creases deeper in her face.

"Why?" I asked.

"Because we need a man here."

For a while, it seemed like things were getting better. Mama didn't look quite so worried. Every morning, Al went to work driving his logging truck, and every night he came home. Mama would have supper ready for him.

Then one night he came home, and supper wasn't ready. Mama had been out in the garden most of the day, getting it ready to plant. She was standing by the stove, cooking something when he came in. He stopped at the door, staring at the empty table.

"Why don't you have supper ready?" he said. His voice was soft, almost a hiss.

"It'll just be a minute. I'm almost done."

Al looked at me, then back at Mama. Then he went to wash up. By the time he got back, mama was putting supper on the table.

I don't know what happened later. I just remember that nobody talked much while we ate. Mama said something, but Al didn't. Later that night, I heard them talking, except it wasn't them talking; it was just Al. The next morning, when Mama was fixing breakfast, I saw the purple bruise on her face.

One day I asked her, "Are you and Al married?"

She shook her head.

"Why not. He lives here."

"Because if we got married, I'd lose my little check."

Then Mama died, and the next chapter was just Al and me. It didn't last long. I knew I had to get away from there, from Al, and I finally did, because I found Miss Erin, and she took me to Miss Ava. So far as most of the people who knew me were concerned, that was when my life really began.

Then I went off to college. Ava hugged me and wiped the tears from her face. She was smiling and crying at the same time. College was another new world, sort of like being born and introduced into the world when you had enough sense to realize it, but not enough to know what to do about it. It took a while to get used to.

Now, every summer, I come up to the cabin. It's Frank Jessup's cabin, the same one that Erin came to. Now it belongs to his wife because Frank died a few years ago. They thought that it would be good for me to spend some time here, just like Erin did.

I don't come here at the same time of the year she did. She was here in the early spring, before things were alive. I come in the summer when the trees are full, and the plants are all green. Everything is alive, and when I sit at the window and look at the world out there, growing and changing, it helps me put what's behind me and what's in front of me together. Maybe, someday, one of those noisy kids in my class will sit somewhere and remember me. Maybe I'll make just a part of the impression on one of them that Miss Erin and Miss Ava made on me.

That's one of the things I pray for.

CPSIA information can be obtained
at www.ICGtesting.com
Printed in the USA
JSHW031118191220
10394JS00002B/125